MW01233633

100 Days ♡ of Thanksgiving

a devotional & journal
from the ♥ of lara love

"Enter into his gates with thanksgiving,
and into his courts with praise:
be thankful unto him, and bless his name."
Psalms 100:4 KJV

www.GoodNews.love

praise the Lord! ——∞∞—— hallelujah!

With all my heart, I ask you to please forgive me! I do my best with scripture(s) references, but am not perfect and also sometimes face technology issues. If there are any mistakes as far as words in italics or bold or verse(s) references or in any other way, I am sorry! Please note I sometimes use brackets […] in verses to add in extra words to help with understanding / application. I encourage you to check verses in your Bible or via an online Bible or via a Bible app on your phone for accuracy and for further study. I committed long ago to read the Bible every day no matter what and to learn to live by it as a totally devoted believer in and follower of the Lord Jesus Christ, and I encourage you with all my heart to do and be the same!

praise the Lord! ————ooo———— hallelujah!

Dedication

Oh Lord, I am sorrier than imaginable

for all the lack of Thanksgiving to you

I have had throughout my life

even in the years I have believed in you

and am learning day by day to follow you!

May this book, dear Father,

be an expression of my Thanksgiving to you!

And may it be an inspiration and encouragement

by your grace for your glory

to all whose hands and hearts

come across it

as well as to me in the writing of it

to learn to truly live

a lifestyle of total devotion to you, oh Lord,

to very much include

having our hearts, mouths, and actions

filled with Thanksgiving to you,

dear Father,

each & every day & forevermore!

With love beyond measure for you, dear God,

Your daughter & servant, Lara

praise the Lord! ——— ∞ ——— hallelujah!

A Little Letter from Lara

Dear friend,

It would be hard to imagine there was ever a more negative, self-pitying, complaining, spoiled, and unthankful person on the planet than I was much if not most of the time FOR DECADES. Even once as an adult in my 20s I placed my faith in Jesus Christ as Lord, and even after some years later I got serious about being a believer in Jesus, and even after some years later I became totally devoted to the Lord and to following Him, and even back when I first started my ministry, I very much lacked Thanksgiving very much of the time. But God has changed me beyond measure!

Now I am not only totally devoted to the Lord and to my ministry work, but I do not want to draw a breath without being, feeling, speaking, and acting with a heart filled with Thanksgiving to God. And when I fall short in this, which I confess I do, I want to repent immediately.

May this book be an encouragement and inspiration to you who read it, and to myself as I write it, to live our lives totally devoted to the Lord with our hearts, our mouths, and our very lives continually filled with Thanksgiving to the Lord – and for the Lord! Hallelujah!

love & blessings,

lara

p.s. I have purposely used an upper case T in Thanksgiving in this book to emphasize the giving of thanks to & for the Lord!

4

Introduction

People in America tend to think of Thanksgiving as a once-a-year holiday marked by time off from work, the beginning of the "holiday season", cooking and baking, turkeys and stuffing and stuffing one's face with endless food, friends, family, fun, football, more food, more fun, and oh yes, still more food, getting ready for the big sales at the stores the day after Thanksgiving Day, putting up Christmas decorations, family traditions, more food, well, you get the point. Somewhere in the mix of it all, toasts may be made at the dinner table and some prayers may be spoken thanking God for His goodness. But all in all, typically what is preeminent for many is not God and Thanksgiving to Him but instead ourselves and enjoying His blessings. The Thanksgiving Day holiday quickly passes, and 364 days now remain until the next celebration of the Thanksgiving Day holiday. As though Thanksgiving does not exist at all or much anyway outside of once a year.

But Thanksgiving in God's eyes isn't about a once-a-year American holiday but is instead about living a life of total devotion to Him to include faith, love, praise, worship, adoration, obedience, service – and THANKSGIVING to the Lord!

The mission of this book is to encourage and inspire us all not to think of Thanksgiving as a once-a-year holiday but to practice a lifestyle of faith in and total devotion to the Lord to blessedly include Thanksgiving to Him each & every day of our lives and forevermore!

How to use this book? Please read on!

How to Use this Book

The most important way to read & use this book is to follow the Lord as He leads you! There are no rules & regulations! I am simply here to share with you love, help, hope, encouragement, & inspiration as the Lord leads me!

What you will find are 100 devotional messages with space for "Journaling". Why just 100? Why not 365? Because the Lord placed upon my heart to write 100 messages to get you started with the hope you will follow the 100 days with a strong commitment to include Thanksgiving to Him as a major component of the rest of your life on this earth and forevermore!

Now a note about the word "Journal". For years, I kept "Journals". Then I was compelled to throw them all away. I had used "Journals" to record what happened in my life, my feelings, my thoughts, details about relationships, how I hurt, how depressed I was, etc. Essentially, the focus was on ME, ME, ME and on what I wanted, what I got, what I lost, whom I lost, how I hurt, how angry I was, feelings, feelings, more and more feelings and more about – and for - me. God has changed me!

Now I write directly into a computer file that is a new kind of "Journal" for me. I actually refer to it at least as of the time of this writing anyway as a "Notebook-Journal". I write there to talk to God, to praise the Lord, to write out prayers, to pour out my heart to God, to record things that have happened in my life, to seek God for wisdom, to write down what I believe He speaks to my heart, to copy scriptures when He places them on my heart, to write ideas for my ministry writing as I wait to see if it's God's will, to write out questions to God and wait for His answers, etc.

For me, the "Notebook-Journal" I keep is no longer all about ME, ME, ME. It is about the Lord and my living totally devoted to Him. And, believe it or not, keeping a "Notebook-Journal" for me is a way of communing with God. It's actually a blessed and beautiful part of my relationship with Him! To me, it's a place my heart meets with God! It's a place I meet with the Lord, yes! Hope my sharing this may inspire you!

I don't want to tell you how to "Journal" in this book or apart from this book. I simply want to encourage you to use the "Journal" space for the glory of God, for you to begin/have/continue on in a forever relationship with Him, for you to grow in your relationship with Him, and hopefully for you to be led to humbly and wholeheartedly express your Thanksgiving to Him on an ongoing basis!

Please note I call the "Journal" space in this book "My Jesus Journal Time" to encourage you to take time each and every day alone in the presence of the Lord to love Him, pray, praise Him, worship Him, sing to Him, study the Bible, seek Him, hear Him, enjoy Him, delight in Him, rest in Him, hope in Him, be corrected by Him, to repent, to grow in Him, be changed by Him, cry out to Him, pour out your heart to Him, etc. – and to "Journal" if you are so led!

I beg you please DO NOT feel this book including your "Jesus Journal Time" needs to be part of your daily alone time with the Lord and the Bible. If the Lord leads you to read and use this in your time with Him, that's great! If not, that's great! What matters more than anything is that you believe in Jesus Christ as Lord, follow Jesus Christ as Lord, and spend time alone with the Lord & the Bible on an ongoing basis!

If this book and your "Jesus Journal time" help, great! If the book and your "Jesus Journal time" do not help, that's fine! Just please be totally devoted to Him and spend time alone in His presence regularly!

Each devotional message I have written is followed by "My Jesus Journal Time". You may fill none of the space, some of the space, or all of the space, and/or you may be led to open a big thick notebook or start a computer file and "Journal". And you may be led to fill up the rest of your life with Journal upon Journal as one of the ways you commune with God and as an ongoing opportunity to love, praise, bless, thank, and glorify Him! Or not. Just please follow the leading of the Lord!

Now, before you dive *into 100 Days of Thanksgiving: a Devotional-Journal from the Heart of Lara Love*, please read the following Very Important Message!

Very Important Message

Before you go forward in this book, or in your life, I ask you with all my heart if you would please read this very important message and make sure what you find within it is at the very foundation of your life going forward! There is truly no more important message in the universe than the one I will share with you now!

God created a perfect world and put people in it so we could have perfect lives and have a perfect forever relationship with Him experiencing and enjoying His love and sharing it with others in perfect relationships with them. But the sins of humanity wrecked this perfect world, wrecked our perfect lives, wrecked the perfect forever relationship with God we were created to have, and wrecked our perfect relationships with others.

Everything wrong in this world is a result of the sins of human beings. The end result is God's wrath at us for our sins, and the punishment we deserve of sin is death, hell, and the lake of fire in forever torment apart from God.

To make a long story short, God loved the world so much He created the one and only way to avoid hell and the lake of fire and to have a relationship with God now and forever in heaven. He sent His only Son Jesus to the earth to lives a perfect sinless life, sent Him to the cross to die to take our sin punishment on Himself, and raised Jesus from the dead. So all who turn from our sins (repent), believe in Jesus Christ as Lord and in His death and resurrection, truly turning our lives over to God and His ways, are forgiven, promised forever life with God, and the Holy Spirit comes to live inside us. When we turn to the Lord and His ways, we are born again spiritually and begin a lifelong journey of believing in and following Jesus.

What does this life of following Jesus look like? In essence, we are to read the Bible and live by it, be filled with God's Spirit and be led by Him, and live totally devoted to the Lord. Loving Him, praising Him, spending time alone with Him, worshiping Him, reading the Bible, seeking God, praying to Him, waiting on Him, hearing Him, obeying Him, serving Him, adoring Him, and bringing Him honor, praise, and glory!

His greatest commands are to love Him with all our hearts AND to love others as ourselves, but this is just the starting place when it comes to others! We are to fellowship with other followers of Jesus as we are all part of the worldwide family of God, God's Kingdom of the children He has adopted when we are spiritually born again into His everlasting family! We are to love one another, share with one another, help one another, encourage one another, pray for one another, support one another in following Jesus, and help bring others into God's Kingdom and help them love and worship and glorify God forever just as we learn to do the same!

For a longer, more detailed explanation and understanding of the Good News (Gospel) message I have just shared with you, and for help following Jesus day by day, please visit my ministry online at www.GoodNews.love where you can read my *Finding the Light* tract which includes my personal story, sign up for my Good News Daily devotional messages sent by email, learn about my ministry, see my special needs ministry dogs, and more. You can also call me at 843-338-2219 or email me at lara@GoodNews.love.

Please pray to God to lead you to a good Lord Jesus Christ-centered, Holy Spirit-filled-and-led, living-according-to-the-Bible church, Bible study, small group, house church, and/or some assembling/gathering of God's people/followers. That you all may love, encourage, pray for, help, and support one other in being totally devoted followers of the Lord Jesus Christ all the while helping still others to become and remain totally devoted followers of the Lord Jesus Christ! All for the glory of God!

Please find below some wonderful Bible verses to help and encourage you regarding this Good News (Gospel) message!

And after the Bible verses, please enjoy *100 Days of Thanksgiving: A Devotional-Journal from the Heart of Lara Love!*

"Jesus said unto him, Thou shalt love the Lord thy God with all thy heart, and with all thy soul, and with all thy mind. This is the first and great commandment. And the second *is* like unto it, Thou shalt love thy neighbour as thyself. On these two commandments hang all the law and the prophets." Matthew 22:37-40

"As it is written, There is none righteous, no, not one:" Romans 3:10

"For all have sinned, and come short of the glory of God;" Romans 3:23

"Let no man deceive you with vain words: for because of these things cometh the wrath of God upon the children of disobedience." Eph. 5:6

"For the wages of sin *is* death; but the gift of God *is* eternal life through Jesus Christ our Lord." Romans 6:23

"The Son of man shall send forth his angels, and they shall gather out of his kingdom all things that offend, and them which do iniquity; And shall cast them into a furnace of fire: there shall be wailing and gnashing of teeth. Then shall the righteous shine forth as the sun in the kingdom of their Father. Who hath ears to hear, let him hear." Mt. 13:41-43

"Jesus answered and said unto him, Verily, verily, I say unto thee, Except a man be born again, he cannot see the kingdom of God. Nicodemus saith unto him, How can a man be born when he is old? can he enter the second time into his mother's womb, and be born? Jesus answered, Verily, verily, I say unto thee, Except a man be born of water and *of* the Spirit, he cannot enter into the kingdom of God. That which is born of the flesh is flesh; and that which is born of the Spirit is spirit." John 3:3-6

"For God so loved the world, that he gave his only begotten Son, that whosoever believeth in him should not perish, but have everlasting life." Jn. 3:16

"That if thou shalt confess with thy mouth the Lord Jesus, and shalt believe in thine heart that God hath raised him from the dead, thou shalt be saved." Romans 10:9

"Then Peter said unto them, Repent, and be baptized every one of you in the name of Jesus Christ for the remission of sins, and ye shall receive the gift of the Holy Ghost." Acts 2:38

"If ye love me, keep my commandments. And I will pray the Father, and he shall give you another Comforter, that he may abide with you for ever; *Even* the Spirit of truth; whom the world cannot receive, because it seeth him not, neither knoweth him: but ye know him; for he dwelleth with you, and shall be in you. I will not leave you comfortless: I will come to you." John 14:15-18

"That we should be to the praise of his glory, who first trusted in Christ. In whom ye also *trusted,* after that ye heard the word of truth, the gospel of your salvation: in whom also after that ye believed, ye were sealed with that holy Spirit of promise, Which is the earnest of our inheritance until the redemption of the purchased possession, unto the praise of his glory." Ephesians 1:12-14

"If ye then, being evil, know how to give good gifts unto your children: how much more shall your heavenly Father give the Holy Spirit to them that ask him?" Luke 11:13

"For as many as are led by the Spirit of God, they are the sons of God." Romans 8:14

"Then said Jesus unto his disciples, If any man will come after me, let him deny himself, and take up his cross, and follow me." Matthew 16:24

"And be not conformed to this world: but be ye transformed by the renewing of your mind, that ye may prove what is that good, and acceptable, and perfect, will of God." Romans 12:2

"Who hath delivered us from the power of darkness, and hath translated *us* into the kingdom of his dear Son:" Colossians 1:13

"Then spake Jesus again unto them, saying, I am the light of the world: he that followeth me shall not walk in darkness, but shall have the light of life." John 8:12

"So then faith *cometh* by hearing, and hearing by the word of God." Romans 10:17

"My sheep hear my voice, and I know them, and they follow me:" John 10:27

"Not every one that saith unto me, Lord, Lord, shall enter into the kingdom of heaven; but he that doeth the will of my Father which is in heaven. Many will say to me in that day, Lord, Lord, have we not prophesied in thy name? and in thy name have cast out devils? and in thy name done many wonderful works? And then will I profess unto them, I never knew you: depart from me, ye that work iniquity." Matthew 7:21-23

"And why call ye me, Lord, Lord, and do not the things which I say?" Luke 6:46

"Grace unto you, and peace, from God our Father and the Lord Jesus Christ. We are bound to thank God always for you, brethren, as it is meet, because that your faith groweth exceedingly, and the charity of every one of you all toward each other aboundeth; So that we ourselves glory in you in the churches of God for your patience and faith in all your persecutions and tribulations that ye endure: *Which is* a manifest token of the righteous judgment of God, that ye may be counted worthy of the kingdom of God, for which ye also suffer: Seeing *it is* a righteous thing with God to recompense tribulation to them that trouble you; And to you who are troubled rest with us, when the Lord Jesus shall be revealed from heaven with his mighty angels, In flaming fire taking vengeance on them that know not God, and that obey not the gospel of our Lord Jesus Christ: Who shall be punished with everlasting destruction from the presence of the Lord, and from the glory of his power; When he shall come to be glorified in his saints, and to be admired in all them that believe (because our testimony among you was believed) in that day. Wherefore also we pray always for you, that our God would count you worthy of *this* calling, and fulfil all the good pleasure of *his* goodness, and the work of faith with power: That the name of our Lord Jesus Christ may be glorified in you, and ye in him, according to the grace of our God and the Lord Jesus Christ." 2 Thessalonians 1:2-12

"And Jesus answered and said unto them, Take heed that no man deceive you. For many shall come in my name, saying, I am Christ; and shall deceive many. And ye shall hear of wars and rumours of wars: see that ye be not troubled: for all *these things* must come to pass, but the end is not yet. For nation shall rise against nation, and kingdom against kingdom: and there shall be famines, and pestilences, and earthquakes, in divers places. All these *are* the beginning of sorrows. Then shall they deliver you up to be afflicted, and shall kill you: and ye shall be hated of all nations for my name's sake. And then shall many be offended, and shall betray one another, and shall hate one another. And many false prophets shall rise, and shall deceive many. And because iniquity shall abound, the love of many shall wax cold. But he that shall endure unto the end, the same shall be saved." Matthew 24:4-13

"And this is life eternal, that they might know thee the only true God, and Jesus Christ, whom thou hast sent." John 17:3

"And *that* he died for all, that they which live should not henceforth live unto themselves, but unto him which died for them, and rose again." 2 Cor. 5:15

Now, onwards! I'm thrilled to have the opportunity now to share with you the devotional messages the Lord placed upon my heart for 100 Days of Thanksgiving!

...

praise the Lord! ——ooo—— hallelujah!

Dear Friend,

Most books begin on an odd page.

I purposely did not

because I wanted the devotional messages

to be lovingly paired

with loads of space

for your Jesus Journal Time!

Please be encouraged!

Please be inspired!

ENJOY!

With the love of Jesus for you & for all,

Lara

#1

Please & Thank You

My beloved parents raised my younger brother and I to have good manners including to say please and thank you, but the big problem was that my family didn't believe in God. We learned how to thank our parents and to thank others, but we didn't learn to thank the Lord for His indescribably amazing goodness. Sadly even when I came to believe in the Lord Jesus Christ, it took me a very long time to realize the most important "manners" are our "manners" with – and most of all our love for and obedience to - God. We should be continually thankful to God, and Thanksgiving to Him should be a part of the very fabric of our hearts and lives! I am convicted even writing this. I have so much growing to do! How about you?

"Enter into his gates with thanksgiving, *and* into his courts with praise: be thankful unto him, *and* bless his name. For the LORD *is* good; his mercy *is* everlasting; and his truth *endureth* to all generations." Psalms 100:4-5 KJV

. . .

praise the Lord! ———∞∞——— hallelujah!

♥ My Jesus Journal Time! ♥

#2

Thankful to Whom?

It's so important in loving others to express our thankfulness to them for their love, kindness, sacrifices, caring, sharing, giving, generosity, etc., but there is no one to whom we should express our Thanksgiving more than the Lord who is the true source of everything good in our lives and on this earth.

Is it not true, though, that we can fall short in thanking God? That we can find ourselves taking Him and His goodness for granted? That we can be so focused on asking that we forget to thank Him for giving? That we can be so busy that we can rush forward in our lives forgetting to thank and praise Him? That we can be like kids on Christmas day tearing through their presents and rushing off to play with them with never a thought of saying thank you for them? Oh, let us take the time each and every day to thank the Lord, to praise and bless His name, to tell Him and show Him how thankful we are!

"Every good gift and every perfect gift is from above, and cometh down from the Father of lights, with whom is no variableness, neither shadow of turning." James 1:17

…

praise the Lord! ———∞∞——— hallelujah!

My Jesus Journal Time!

#3

Thankful for the Giver!

A loved one long ago warned me to not be more focused on the gifts than the Giver, but truth is I have done that more times than I care to remember. Of course we should be exceedingly thankful for every single blessing God bestows upon us on this earth. But there is truly no greater gift, no greater blessing, than God Himself, than God sending His only Son Jesus Christ to the cross to die to pay our sin penalty and to raise Him from the dead, and than the promise of forever life with God through repentance and turning our hearts and lives over to God and His ways.

The Lord Himself, and everlasting life with Him, is the greatest gift we can ever have. Yet if you're anything like I am, sometimes I become so focused on what I have from God and what I desire from God and what I am praying to receive from God that I lose sight of being thankful above all else for God Himself and forever and ever with Him! May this be a reminder to us all concerning Thanksgiving that there is no greater gift than God! Thank you Lord!

"For God so loved the world, that he gave his only begotten Son, that whosoever believeth in him should not perish, but have everlasting life. For God sent not his Son into the world to condemn the world; but that the world through him might be saved." John 3:16-17 KJV

...

praise the Lord! ———ᴏᴏᴏ——— hallelujah!

❤ My Jesus Journal Time! ❤

#4

Spiritual Blessings!

Not only is God our greatest gift, and not only is God the giver of every wonderful gift, but God isn't just the giver of physical blessings! God, as the Bible shows us, is the giver of every single "spiritual blessing". Have you ever considered this, and have you ever expressed your Thanksgiving to God for all your spiritual blessings?

I can't speak for God, so I don't want to assume I know exactly what all of His spiritual blessings are. But when I think of spiritual blessings, I like to think of beautiful blessings like love, hope, joy, peace, kindness, mercy, grace, forgiveness, compassion, communing with God, friendship with God, loving relationships with people, wisdom from God, the Truth of the Bible, etc. Hoping this message inspires you to think of your spiritual blessings and to be thankful to God for them!

"Blessed *be* the God and Father of our Lord Jesus Christ, who hath blessed us with all spiritual blessings in heavenly *places* in Christ:" Ephesians 1:3 KJV

…

praise the Lord! ——————ooo—————— hallelujah!

My Jesus Journal Time!

praise the Lord! ———·οοο·——— *hallelujah!*

#5

Being Thankful

Have you ever expressed being thankful to someone even though in your heart you didn't feel thankful? In other words, have you felt obligated to say thank you to be polite but were anything but thankful inside of you? Like you just wanted to get the "thank you" over with and move on with your life? Whether or not that person could tell you weren't really thankful is not what this message is about. It's about you and me and God.

God sees inside our hearts. He knows us inside and out. He knows every one of our thoughts and knows our feelings, too. When God looks inside your heart, does He see Thanksgiving? Does He see a thankful person? Is Thanksgiving part of your way of life? Don't you think this matters to God? Oh, I believe it must matter so very greatly. I want God to look inside my heart and to see love, joy, and Thanksgiving on an ongoing basis. And I want Him to lead me to repentance when my heart is all wrong. How about you?

"I the LORD search the heart, *I* try the reins [per Strong's concordance also "mind"], even to give every man according to his ways, *and* according to the fruit of his doings." Jeremiah 17:10 KJV

…

praise the Lord! ———○○○——— hallelujah!

My Jesus Journal Time!

#6

Inside Your Mind

If there is any place in my life that needs constant cleansing, growth, refining, purification, and transformation, it's my mind! I have such a very long history of negativity, complaining, whining, self-pity, criticism, pride, judgment, condemnation, discouragement, self-centeredness, etc. it's a wonder the Lord ever picked someone like me to start a ministry and proclaim Him to the world! God has His work cut out for Him to say the least, and I might say He is doing an amazing work in me considering how He is continually teaching, testing, and growing me.

You know, I believe with all my heart that Thanksgiving to God should not simply be pouring out of our mouths and ever evident in our actions. I believe Thanksgiving should fill our minds. I believe God's people should be people of faith and love without a doubt – and people of Thanksgiving. Right down to our thoughts. God has been teaching me over the years to get rid of the negativity when I fall into it and to replace the wrong thoughts with godly ones. With good ones. Righteous ones. God-honoring ones. To very much include thoughts that show forth Thanksgiving to God. Are your thoughts filled with Thanksgiving?

"Casting down imaginations, and every high thing that exalteth itself against the knowledge of God, and bringing into captivity every thought to the obedience of Christ;" 2 Corinthians 10:5 KJV

...

praise the Lord! —————∞∞∞————— hallelujah!

♥ My Jesus Journal Time! ♥

#7

When Pride Prevents Thanksgiving

When we're proud in our hearts, our words, and our actions, all of which is sin, we pat ourselves on the back and magnify ourselves and take the glory for the good in our lives. We think, say, and act like it's our hard work, it's our accomplishments, it's our resumes, it's our connections, it's our provision, etc. that results in the good in our lives. Instead of thanking God for His love, His goodness, His greatness, His provision, His resources, His connecting us to different people, programs, etc., we take all the credit ourselves. So instead of being thankful to God, we puff ourselves up in our own minds and glorify ourselves in the ears and sight of others rather than praising the Lord and thanking Him!

The quick and necessary fix concerning pride is repentance, humbling ourselves, and exalting and glorifying – and thanking – God. Have some repenting and humbling yourself to do?

"Every one *that is* proud in heart *is* an abomination to the LORD: *though* hand *join* in hand, he shall not be unpunished." Proverbs 16:5 KJV

. . .

praise the Lord! ———∞∞——— hallelujah!

♥ My Jesus Journal Time! ♥

#8

More than Words

I believe with all my heart there is a way to practice Thanksgiving to God on an ongoing basis that is far greater than merely telling God over and again, "Thank you God! Thank you God!" Oh, most assuredly, I believe we should absolutely tell the Lord regularly how much we love Him and how thankful we are to Him for Him first and foremost as well as for all His endless blessings. But words are words, and I believe we can do something that "speaks" beyond words.

I believe we can SHOW God how much we love Him and how thankful we are to Him in our actions by lovingly obeying Him including serving Him! Each and every day, we can choose to humble ourselves and in our decision-making to choose to do what brings God love, honor, praise, joy, pleasure, honor, and glory. We can "thank God", in essence, in our obedience and service to Him.

Have you considered obedience including service to God as an expression of love for and Thanksgiving to Him? I encourage you to SHOW the Lord your love and Thanksgiving daily!

I love in the following little Bible story how Peter's mother-in-law responded to Jesus healing her with serving. Do you suppose she did so with a thankful heart? I would most certainly think so!

"And when Jesus was come into Peter's house, he saw his wife's mother laid, and sick of a fever. And he touched her hand, and the fever left her: and she arose, and ministered unto them." Matthew 8:14-15 KJV

...

praise the Lord! ⎯⎯⎯⎯∞⎯⎯⎯⎯ hallelujah!

♥ My Jesus Journal Time! ♥

#9

Staying Thankful

Being thankful is one thing. Staying thankful is another, isn't it? It is for me anyway. Sometimes I find my heart so filled with Thanksgiving to God. Then I allow myself to get weighed down with struggles, stresses, worries, troubles, challenges, etc. Next thing I know there isn't an ounce of Thanksgiving in my heart let alone coming out of my mouth or in my actions. What do you suppose it would take to stay thankful?

I believe staying thankful has to do with learning to keep our focus on the Lord, on the Bible, on His ways and will for us, and above all else on His amazingness, awesomeness, magnificence, goodness, greatness, blessings, etc. For those of us like myself who have trouble keeping our focus and are easily distracted, it can be a big challenge to stay focused. And to get re-focused when we lose our focus. Whether it's easy for us or hard, let's strive to focus on the Lord and to ever be thankful to Him!

Hope these verses encourage you as much as they encourage me!

"If ye then be risen with Christ, seek those things which are above, where Christ sitteth on the right hand of God. Set your affection [also "exercise the mind" per Strong's concordance] on things above, not on things on the earth." Colossians 3:1-2 KJV

...

praise the Lord! ———ꝏ——— hallelujah!

My Jesus Journal Time!

#10

Praying with Thanksgiving

Something I find totally wild when it comes to praying is how God calls us to pray of all things WITH THANKSGIVING. Doesn't it seem strange to you that God wants us to pray WITH THANKSGIVING when we don't even know if He will answer our prayers the way we want Him to answer them? Why, and how, can we pray like this? I personally believe the "why" is simple. We should do what God tells us in the Bible to do. What about the "how"? I believe when we put our trust in Him, and remind ourselves that God always knows what is best, we can thank Him in advance of answering our prayers. We can thank Him for His will in the matter we are praying about as well as in all matters! I still have such a long way to go in trusting the Lord, and I tend to forget to thank the Lord when I pray to Him. May this message be a reminder to us all!

"Be careful for nothing; but in every thing by prayer and supplication with thanksgiving let your requests be made known unto God. And the peace of God, which passeth all understanding, shall keep your hearts and minds through Christ Jesus." Philippians 4:6-7 KJV

"Continue in prayer, and watch [also "keep awake" or "be vigilant" per Strong's concordance] in the same with thanksgiving;" Colossians 4:2 KJV

...

praise the Lord! ———∞∞——— hallelujah!

♥ My Jesus Journal Time! ♥

#11

Alone with the Lord!

I can't think of a more beautiful and precious and intimate time when it comes to Thanksgiving to God than spending time alone with Him praising and worshiping Him and thanking Him for whatever is on our hearts for which to thank Him! The more I follow Jesus, the less I have found enjoyment in the typical worldly enjoyments of this life on earth. But something I find enjoyable more than words can say is taking walks in the fresh air with God praising Him, praying to Him, singing to Him, seeking Him, hearing Him, repenting when I need to repent, asking Him for direction, pouring out my heart to Him, and showing Him my Thanksgiving in my heart, out of my mouth, and in the delight I find in spending time alone with Him!

I so very much encourage you to find time each and every day to spend alone with God, with the Bible, rejoicing in His presence and expressing to Him your Thanksgiving! Come away from the busyness of this life! Come away and spend time alone with the Lord! Show and tell Him how very, very, very thankful you are in your time alone with Him and throughout the day and night even in the time that you have not set apart for just you and Him!

"My beloved spake, and said unto me, Rise up, my love, my fair one, and come away." Song of Solomon 2:10 KJV

...

praise the Lord! —————ooo————— hallelujah!

♥ My Jesus Journal Time! ♥

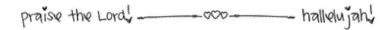

praise the Lord! ——ooo—— hallelujah!

#12

Tell the World About Him!

It would be hard for me to imagine anything would mean more to the Lord in the way of Thanksgiving than when we come into His presence and burst forth with heartfelt Thanksgiving, but the Bible makes clear there is another wonderful way to pour out our Thanksgiving to the Lord. And that is to tell the world about Him! We can share the Gospel message, we can point people to Him, we can help people understand and live by the Bible, we can love them and encourage them and pray for them and such, and we can proclaim to them His wondrousness and marvelousness and phenomenal-ness with glad, joyful, thankful hearts! Please be inspired in reading the following verse!

"Give thanks unto the LORD, call upon his name, make known his deeds among the people." 1 Samuel 16:8 KJV

"That I may publish with the voice of thanksgiving, and tell of all thy wondrous works." Psalms 26:7

...

praise the Lord! ————∞∞———— hallelujah!

♥ My Jesus Journal Time! ♥

#13

Thanksgiving with Others

I wonder if God ever gets tired of Thanksgiving. Surely not. He is worthy of praise, honor, glory, and Thanksgiving forever and ever. So may we be people of Thanksgiving, and may we not miss opportunities to thank the Lord nor miss the various ways in which we can offer Him thanks. Thanking God when we're on our own is so very vital, but then so is thanking the Lord in the company of others. God makes clear we who follow Him should not forsake assembling together, and is this not a perfect opportunity to join together in Thanksgiving? Oh, yes!

I confess to you so many times I have attended church services and joined in singing to and praising God as more of a religious activity than an amazing opportunity to thank the Lord with all my heart. I am here to encourage you and to encourage myself to see coming together with other believers in Jesus whether in formal ways like in a church service or in more personal informal ways like standing on a street corner or going out for a cup of coffee or talking and praying together on the telephone as opportunities to thank the Lord as His children, as fellow followers, as people dedicated to giving God the praise, honor, glory, and Thanksgiving He is due!

"Not forsaking the assembling of ourselves together, as the manner of some *is;* but exhorting *one another:* and so much the more, as ye see the day approaching." Hebrews 10:25 KJV

"I will give thee thanks in the great congregation: I will praise thee among much people." Psalms 35:18 KJV

...

praise the Lord! ———∞∞——— hallelujah!

My Jesus Journal Time!

#14

An Unbelievable Testimony

If I hadn't witnessed this myself, it would be very hard to believe. But God richly blessed me with giving me two precious friends who both had major cancer at the same time. They lived very far apart, but He led me to introduce them by phone and email. They became good friends and supported each other through unimaginable challenges as the cancer sought to destroy their lives. They both were strong believers in the Lord Jesus Christ, and they both had amazing peace through their trials as they knew they would survive the cancer and have more time on earth with God with them here or they would go to heaven and be with God there.

Their battles with cancer ended the same. They both died. And what stood out to me more than anything was the amazing love, joy, and THANKSGIVING they had all the way until the end! I never heard them complain. I never heard them angry at God. They were humbly and simply thankful to God for being their God, Lord, King, and Savior, and for all His blessings throughout their lives. I am so humbled. I am known to moan and groan and be self-pitying over the smallest of my matters. I have such a long, long way to go and grow when it comes to Thanksgiving. And I am resolved to do just that. To continue to grow in love, humility, joy, and Thanksgiving. Oh, let us grow!

...

praise the Lord! ———∞∞——— hallelujah!

♥ My Jesus Journal Time! ♥

#15
Thankful Dogs!

Having done about 20 years or so of intensive dog rescue work including having had in my care numerous special needs dogs and having had a sanctuary-like setting in my home environment for some years, I can honestly say I have seen countless dogs up close and personal with which God entrusted me show a love, trust, joy, peace, and Thanksgiving no matter what they went through.

Not that they could speak, mind you. Not that they were believers in and followers of the Lord Jesus Christ as humans are called to be. Not that they read the Bible and praised and worshiped the Lord to no end. But there was, and with the last of my special needs ministry dogs in my care now, remains a simple, sweet, disposition and appearance and attitude of Thanksgiving to their Creator, God, and to me, their Mommie and caregiver and for their little simple and precious lives.

How convicting, and humbling, that so many dogs that have passed through my life have done a better job than I have of living what in my estimate was/is a lifestyle of love, trust, and Thanksgiving. I am most assuredly a work in progress ever in need of more humility, more purification, and more growth – and more love, joy & Thanksgiving! And you?

"Being confident of this very thing, that he which hath begun a good work in you will perform *it* until the day of Jesus Christ:" Philippians 1:6 KJV

...

praise the Lord! ———ooo——— hallelujah!

♥ My Jesus Journal Time! ♥

#16

Food, Clothing & Shelter

Though my life has been filled with seemingly relentless pretty big challenges of one sort or another, I have been so incredibly blessed to always have had food, clothing, and shelter while so many people worldwide have gone without. So sadly, however, I took this for granted for such a very long time. Now, I try not to take a single blessing for granted. I am thankful for every ounce of food, every article of clothing, and every roof over my head I have ever had.

What changed me? God did. He is teaching me day by day to love and serve Him with all my heart, to love others as myself, to live utterly for Him, and to be thankful for all with which He blesses me day by day. Some people take credit for food, clothing, shelter, and their other provision and blessings as though they earn and deserve it as a result of their resumes, work experience, jobs, etc. I don't take credit for food, shelter, clothing, or any other blessing in my life no matter how hard I work. I give God all the glory, and I am thankful to God beyond measure for every blessing I have ever had, have now, or will ever have.

I am also thankful to the people God has placed in my life over the years most especially my family who have been so loving and generous and giving and helpful whereby God has often provided for me and blessed me through others. And I believe thanking people is so very important. But the one who should be thanked above anyone in the universe is the Lord! May we never take for granted God's goodness, and may we be ever thankful to Him as well as to those through whom He is so good to us! And may we be thankful to Him for them! ALL – absolutely ALL – the glory TO THE LORD for all the good in our lives!

"The LORD *is* my shepherd; I shall not want." Psalms 23:1

"But my God shall supply all your need according to his riches in glory by Christ Jesus." Philippians 4:19 KJV

…

praise the Lord! ———♡♡♡——— hallelujah!

♥ My Jesus Journal Time! ♥

praise the Lord! ———ooo——— hallelujah!

#17

Taking Nothing for Granted

Not only have I taken the big things in life for granted like food, clothing, and shelter, but I have also taken little things for granted not to mention everything between big and little. Nothing, absolutely nothing, and nobody, absolutely nobody, with which and with whom God blesses us should be taken for granted. From a bit of sunshine on a rainy day to being able to feel the sand between our toes on the beach to being able to walk when so many people can't walk to being healthy after a sickness to being able to think and speak and write to having vision to being able to afford glasses when we need them to living in a country in which we can own a Bible and read it to having family and friends to being able to breathe to drinking a glass of fresh clean water when so many don't have access to clean water or any water at all to having a job to having someone pray for us, etc., all of these are gifts and blessings from God we should never take for granted!

Makes you think, doesn't it? Is there anything in our lives right now, or anyone, we've been taking for granted? What a wonderful opportunity we have every breath of our lives to praise the Lord, to worship the Lord, to thank the Lord, for who He is, for what He has done, is doing, and will do, for all of His spiritual and physical blessings, most of all for God Himself and for His love and salvation and for forever with Him for those of us who have repented and received Jesus Christ as Lord! Oh, praise the Lord! Thank you God! Forever and ever, thank the Lord!

"Bless the LORD, O my soul: and all that is within me, *bless* his holy name. Bless the LORD, O my soul, and forget not all his benefits:" Psalms 103:1-2 KJV

"Who covereth the heaven with clouds, who prepareth rain for the earth, who maketh grass to grow upon the mountains." Psalms 147:8 KJV

...

praise the Lord! ————♡♡♡———— hallelujah!

My Jesus Journal Time!

#18

Living for the Lord

One of my favorite verses in the Bible, and one that for me sums up the way God created us all to live, which you will find below, is what I think of as the ultimate way to have a heart and life filled with Thanksgiving to God. When we can honestly say we are living and breathing to love and glorify God, when we are sincerely totally devoted to Him, when Jesus truly is our first love and there is nothing we desire more than the Lord and living for Him, when we yearn to live to love, honor, praise, adore, worship, serve, obey, and glorify Him more than anything else, when we want to love and serve God not to love and serve self, I believe we are expressing to God our Thanksgiving! Where do you stand with this? Are you living for the Lord?

"And *that* he died for all, that they which live should not henceforth live unto themselves, but unto him which died for them, and rose again." 2 Corinthians 5:15 KJV

...

praise the Lord! ———∘∞∘——— hallelujah!

❤ My Jesus Journal Time! ❤

#19

Indescribably Thankful

There is nothing and nobody in the world I am thankful for more than I am thankful for the Lord Himself. And than for my forever relationship with Him He has given me through repentance and believing in Jesus Christ as Lord and in His death and resurrection and truly committing my heart and life to God and His ways. I am indescribably thankful for so much, but I am indescribably thankful above all else for the Lord.

I am totally devoted to Him. And the more I follow Him, and the more time I spend alone in His presence, the more I read the Bible and live by it, the more I am filled with and led by the Holy Spirit, the more I humble myself and live for God not for self, the more I fall in love with the Lord, the deeper my relationship with Him, and the more thankful I am for Him.

I am quite sure forever will not be enough for me to tell God how thankful I am to Him – for Him. I hope this message inspires you to be thankful to God – for God – more than you are thankful for anything or anyone in the universe! Hallelujah!

"I will bless the LORD at all times: his praise *shall* continually *be* in my mouth." Psalms 34:1 KJV

...

praise the Lord! ——ooo—— hallelujah!

My Jesus Journal Time!

praise the Lord! ———ooo——— hallelujah!

#20

The Midnight Hour

When I was quickly scanning through a list of Bible verses about being thankful, I was strongly drawn to a verse I am sure I must have read over the years but to which I had never paid any serious attention. Immediately I was struck by it. Moved would be a more accurate word. Deeply, deeply moved in fact.

You will see in the verse below how the psalmist makes a conscious decision to wake up in the middle of the night TO THANK THE LORD! Now if you're anything like I am, I need my sleep. And truth is I haven't slept super well in many years. The idea of purposely getting up in the middle of the night my self-centered flesh would not even consider. And though I do wake in the middle of the night on a regular basis, much of the time I try desperately to fall back asleep though I have come to believe God wakes me on purpose to spend time with Him and the Bible and pray and such as I am so easily distracted during the daytime.

Truth is even when I do quit trying to fall back asleep and spend time with God, I am not sure I ever considered using some of that middle-of-the-night time to thank and praise the Lord – until the Lord opened my heart and eyes to the verse. I wonder if perhaps the Lord might use this same verse in your life to encourage you to consider the midnight hours to thank the Lord!

"At midnight I will rise to give thanks unto thee because of thy righteous judgments." Psalms 119:62

...

praise the Lord! ——————ooo—————— hallelujah!

My Jesus Journal Time!

#21

Three Times Daily

I have known for years that the prophet Daniel prayed diligently and decidedly multiple times daily per the Bible, but not until I started writing this book and looked up verses related to Thanksgiving did I find the verse below – and was I moved to the start of tears in reading it.

I had always assumed Daniel simply prayed to ask God for what it was he wanted. What I had missed was that Daniel prayed – AND GAVE THANKS! Oh, hallelujah! How could I have missed that? Honestly? Because I am by nature so self-consumed that I have usually thought of prayer as ASKING, ASKING, and ASKING God instead of thinking of prayer as simply communing with God in a number of ways – including THANKING HIM!

While I am someone who is led to pray day and night without any set schedule, I have sorely lacked when it comes to Thanksgiving. This is an area where I need so much humility and growth. What an inspiration and encouragement the following verse is for us to spend time alone in the presence of God and to pray to Him – and to THANK HIM. Oh, praise the Lord! Let us praise, praise, praise and thank the Lord, AMEN!

"Now when Daniel knew that the writing was signed, he went into his house; and his windows being open in his chamber toward Jerusalem, he kneeled upon his knees three times a day, and prayed, and gave thanks before his God, as he did aforetime." Daniel 6:10 KJV

...

praise the Lord! —————ᴏᴏᴏ————— hallelujah!

My Jesus Journal Time!

#22

Thanksgiving for Others

The apostle Paul didn't just pray to God for people, as I believe we are all called to do, but he THANKED GOD for people! What an inspiration! How often do we take the time to thank God for the people in our lives? And when we do, do we restrict our giving of thanks to God concerning our closest friends and family members? Or do we thank Him for ALL the people who come in and out of our lives?

If we truly took the time to thank God for all that we should thank Him for, I daresay forever would not be enough! Let us remember when it comes to Thanksgiving to thank God for the people He weaves in and out of our lives from the nice lady at the grocery store register to the person who cleans the toilets in our office building to the church pastor to the mean people God puts in our path to test us to absolutely anyone and everyone, oh, let us thank the Lord for the people in our lives!

Should this in fact include our spouses, children, grandchildren, parents, co-workers, employers, accountants, teachers, etc.? Absolutely! But may we never limit our giving of thanks when it comes to people nor when it comes to giving of thanks for absolutely anything at all. God is worthy of our Thanksgiving 24-7 – forevermore!

"Cease not to give thanks for you, making mention of you in my prayers;" Ephesians 1:16

...

praise the Lord! ———ooo——— hallelujah!

My Jesus Journal Time!

#23

Abounding with Thanksgiving

God has gifted me in words. Writing them. Speaking them. Paying close attention to them. Noticing them. Being moved by God through them. Sometimes speaking and writing too many. Sometimes speaking and writing too few. Sometimes speaking and writing the wrong ones. Sometimes the right ones. When other people are preoccupied with other things, it is likely I may be preoccupied with words. Of course, the greatest when it comes to words is the Bible, God's Word. And how delighted I was when I began working on my *100 Days of Thanksgiving* book to come across a very powerful word in the verse below. *Abounding.*

I like to think of abounding as being so filled that something or someone is overflowing. The content cannot be contained. Something is so big that it cannot be held back. To what does the word abounding refer in the verse to follow? Thanksgiving! The apostle Paul tells the people – and us – to be rooted and built up in the Lord Jesus Christ, to be established in our faith in Him, and to ABOUND WITH THANKSGIVING!

Am I? Are you? Oh, let us be! Amen!

"As ye have therefore received Christ Jesus the Lord, *so* walk ye in him: Rooted and built up in him, and stablished in the faith, as ye have been taught, abounding therein with thanksgiving." Colossians 2:6-7 KJV

...

praise the Lord! ———ooo——— hallelujah!

♥ My Jesus Journal Time! ♥

#24

Singing with Thanksgiving!

If you've read my writing for Jesus for any period of time, which usually includes personal testimony as I help people to become and remain totally devoted followers of the Lord Jesus Christ, you have more than likely learned about how I believe I must have the worst singing voice ever. And I am NOT someone who likes to sing – at all. I don't even care much for music as I used to. But when it comes to singing to the Lord, I LOVE going on walks in the fresh air and praising and worshiping and singing to God and praying to Him, pouring out my heart to Him, repenting when I need to, and seeking Him and hearing Him and enjoying His sweet blessed holy company. I love how God through the following verse encourages us to sing to Him – with Thanksgiving. Will you?

"Sing unto the LORD with thanksgiving; sing praise upon the harp unto our God:" Psalms 147:7

...

praise the Lord! ———ᴑᴑᴑ——— hallelujah!

My Jesus Journal Time!

#25

Joyful Sounds of Thanksgiving!

Some people like really quiet church services. Some people like loud ones. I really don't think church should be about what we like and don't like. What does God desire? I would imagine more than anything He wants our hearts and lives totally devoted to Him and that this be reflected whether we're in the church building or outside of it. As far as quiet church services or loud ones or anything in between, I would think what God desires most is that everything about the services including the music be about showing Him love, honor, praise, worship, and glory and helping others to do the same.

As far as noise, some believe God would only want to be worshiped and revered in a really quiet way. Truth is the Bible makes clear that joyful and yes even loud noises and sounds and song and musical instruments WHEN THEY ARE MEANT TO GLORIFY HIM bless Him!

Whether or not we are in a church service, wherever we are when we worship God, let us never hold back our praise, honor, song, sounds, and any other manner in which we express our Thanksgiving to God and glorify Him with every ounce of our hearts, mouths, and lives!

"Make a joyful noise unto God, all ye lands:" Psalms 66:1

"Sing aloud unto God our strength: make a joyful noise unto the God of Jacob." Psalms 81:1

"O come, let us sing unto the LORD: let us make a joyful noise to the rock of our salvation." Psalms 95:1

"Make a joyful noise unto the LORD, all the earth: make a loud noise, and rejoice, and sing praise." Psalms 98:4

"With trumpets and sound of cornet make a joyful noise before the LORD, the King." Psalms 98:6

…

praise the Lord! ——♡♡♡—— hallelujah!

My Jesus Journal Time!

praise the Lord! ⸺ ∞ ⸺ hallelujah!

#26

Sacrifice of Thanksgiving

God shows us in the Bible we should offer to Him the "sacrifice of Thanksgiving", but how can Thanksgiving be a sacrifice? I can't speak for God, but this is what comes to my heart. First, long ago, when people were under the law and Jesus Christ Savior of the world had not yet come to the earth, died on the cross, and been raised from the dead, there was an extremely serious and involved system of making sacrifices to God. So the "sacrifice of Thanksgiving" could simply be a reference to the system of sacrifices when people were under the law. But what also comes to my heart is that the flesh must make a "sacrifice" in getting the focus off of self and onto God, in turning away from our self-centered thoughts, desires, activities, etc., and taking the time to focus on God, and on the Bible, and on THANKING HIM!

I may never have a full understanding of the "sacrifice of Thanksgiving", but I do know this. We should make this "sacrifice" without fail each and every day no matter the cost to our flesh. No matter what and whom we need to lay aside to spend time in God's presence loving and praising Him, thanking and worshiping Him, honoring and glorifying Him, we should make that "sacrifice" and turn our hearts, mouths, eyes, and very lives to the Lord with hearts filled with love, adoration, and Thanksgiving! And our Thanksgiving to God should not be limited to our alone time with Him. Every aspect of our hearts and lives should be overflowing with our Thanksgiving!

…

praise the Lord! ———∞∞———— hallelujah!

♥ My Jesus Journal Time! ♥

#27

Thankful in Retrospect

At times I have looked back at my life and seen that the very things, circumstances, people, relationships, challenges, trials, tribulations, struggles, hurdles, obstacles, hard times, brokenness, world events, etc. that I felt so miserable about I allowed to keep me in a place of bondage to myself wherein I missed amazing opportunities to be thankful to God. Only in retrospect, by the grace of God, with the Holy Spirit illuminating the truth, have I been able to look back and see how thankful I could and should have been had I had a different attitude and perspective – and had I humbled myself and truly put my full trust in the Lord.

Now, in my looking back, I have had Thanksgiving to God because of all He did back then in me, through me, with me, in the world, in others' lives, etc.

I wish I were perfect. I wish I were more mature. I wish I had stronger trust in God and faith in Him. I wish I would have been thankful to the Lord all along. Oh, but God is so merciful. And as He grows me, He is teaching me to be thankful on an ongoing basis. Such that I no longer need to do so much looking back to see the Thanksgiving I missed in the past. Because now I am at long last learning how to be thankful – daily.

Oh, He is so merciful! Let us not neglect to be thankful to God, not ever. No matter the circumstances of our lives. Let us be thankful to the Lord. This very breath. And the next one, let us praise God. And let us be thankful to the Lord God almighty – everlastingly. Amen!

. . .

praise the Lord! ———∞∞————— hallelujah!

♥ My Jesus Journal Time! ♥

praise the Lord! ⸻ooo⸻ hallelujah!

#28

Complaining Isn't Thanksgiving

May seem obvious to you, but complaining isn't Thanksgiving. And some of us very much including myself need to do a much better job of owning up to complaining, repenting from it, and choosing Thanksgiving to God instead! Unfortunately for those of us well-versed at neglecting to see our sin or refusing to acknowledge it and simply continuing on with it can go on for years doing the same wrong thing and neglecting to do what is right.

My confession? For years, I complained, whined, moaned, groaned, and felt sorry for myself as I dragged zillions of others into my self-centered sinful mess. Thanks be to God for I can take no credit for this whatsoever, I am now able to recognize when I fall into complaining more and more quickly and try really hard to repent quickly and to resume learning to live my life filled with Thanksgiving.

When our hearts, mouths, and actions are filled with complaining, how could we possibly have room for Thanksgiving? Let's stop our complaining. May our hearts, words, and actions be marked not by once-in-a-while thankfulness to God but by continual Thanksgiving to the Lord most high!

"Do all things without murmurings [complaining in some Bible versions] and disputings:" Philippians 2:14 KJV

...

praise the Lord! ———— ∞∞ ———— hallelujah!

♥ My Jesus Journal Time! ♥

#29

Repenting for Un-thankfulness

I used to think repenting means we simply say sorry to God and ask for His forgiveness. Then we feel good because He forgives us. Then we go back to the wrong we were doing because we can't help it of course or at least I couldn't anyway. Then we ask Him to forgive us again. An endless circle of saying sorry and returning over and again to the very same sin we should have left behind.

Going by this, when it comes to lacking Thanksgiving, shouldn't we just have to tell God sorry for being unthankful, get His forgiveness, maybe try being thankful a little bit, and then obviously resort right back to lacking Thanksgiving? This is not how Jesus' followers are to live. We are to learn in the strength of Christ for the glory of Christ to leave sin behind. And so it is un-thankfulness should truly become a thing of the past. And more and more, we should be resolved that our hearts, words, and lives shine with ongoing Thanksgiving. I'm working on this. Want to join me?

...

praise the Lord! ——— ∞ ——— hallelujah!

♥ My Jesus Journal Time! ♥

#30

The Gratitude Game

Long ago someone told me about "the gratitude game". It seemed like an easy game but it wasn't so easy to play. I was to go through the alphabet from A to Z and think of something I was grateful for beginning with each letter. There were a few big problems with the way I played.

First of all, I knew very little about the Lord and the Bible at that time from what I recall so I thought of gratitude as essentially just being grateful for whatever or whomever without any real understanding of being THANKFUL TO GOD. Second, for the most part, I was an extremely unthankful person.

Oh, times have changed. Now I know everything in this life for which we should be grateful comes from God. And His love and goodness are simply endless! Many years ago I was introduced to "god" as a "higher power" I could choose based on my own desires and beliefs. I was told I could choose an ocean, a doorknob, anything or anyone that was "higher" than me. Gratitude then would be about being grateful to whomever my "higher power" was. Oh, how deceived I was!

There is one true God, God almighty who is Father, Jesus the Son, and the Holy Ghost in one, and our "gratitude" should be endless Thanksgiving to God almighty in Christ. Hallelujah! Perhaps you'll be led to go through the alphabet making a list of blessings for which you are thankful to the Lord! I love, love, love to reflect on the Lord, the Bible, and all that I'm thankful to God for. Most of all when it comes to Thanksgiving, I love to praise and thank the Lord! Hope you do too!

…

praise the Lord! ———∞∞——— hallelujah!

My Jesus Journal Time!

#31

God's Longsuffering

Even after years of trying to faithfully follow Jesus, I still fall terribly far short when it comes to patience. My lack of patience makes me even more in awe of God's phenomenal patience with humanity. In the King James version of the Bible, patience is sometimes referred to as "longsuffering". This makes so much sense to me because there is a suffering in patiently waiting for something or someone.

In God's case, He could and should have given up on humanity long, long ago. But in His exceeding love for us, He not only sent His only Son Jesus to the cross to die to pay our sin penalty and to be raised from the dead, but He continues to this very day to give this world more time to repent and turn to Jesus Christ as Lord. This world is running out of time for sure, but as of yet God is still amazingly longsuffering. I believe we as humans are quick to be thankful for our physical possessions, but let us not forget to give God our Thanksgiving for His astonishingly beautiful and powerful attributes. Including His longsuffering.

In addition to being thankful to God for His unsurpassable longsuffering with all of humanity, let us ever be thankful for His immeasurable patience with each of His children as we are continually in need of more of His love, grace, kindness, mercy, help, etc. We don't deserve any of His patience, do we? But oh, He is so lovingly gloriously mercifully longsuffering!

"The Lord is not slack concerning his promise, as some men count slackness; but is longsuffering to us-ward, not willing that any should perish, but that all should come to repentance." 2 Peter 3:9 KJV

...

praise the Lord! ———∞∞——— hallelujah!

♥ My Jesus Journal Time! ♥

#32

God's Grace

After decades of dog rescue work, as I write this book I am down to my last two special needs ministry dogs. I had 19 at one time! I didn't choose who would live the longest nor who would be adopted out and who would remain with me. God did! I have done my best to pray and follow Him! A friend pointed out to me the names of my last remaining dogs. Miss Mercy and Grace. Yes, that's right. Mercy and Grace!

I love to tell people when I do streets and beach ministry my dogs' names. I say this. "Their names are Miss Mercy like "Lord have mercy." And Grace like "God's grace." Praising God forever would still be insufficient given all the reasons God is worthy of our praise and Thanksgiving, and some of these reasons stand out to me more than others. Like His love, His mercy, and His grace!

Some say grace is "undeserved favor". I am not an expert in definitions, but I can say this. I am blown away by the enormity of His grace that He would give everlasting life to all who turn from our sins, believe in Jesus Christ as Lord and Savior and in His death and resurrection, truly turning our lives over to God and His ways. We could never ever earn God's love, grace, and everlasting life with Him. Nonetheless He gives it to us by His grace through faith in and our lives being devoted to the Lord Jesus Christ. How could we ever thank the Lord enough for His astonishingly wonderfully blessed beautiful glorious grace?

"For by grace are ye saved through faith; and that not of yourselves: *it is* the gift of God: Not of works, lest any man should boast. For we are his workmanship, created in Christ Jesus unto good works, which God hath before ordained that we should walk in them." Ephesians 2:8-10 KJV

...

praise the Lord! ——————◦◦◦—————— hallelujah!

~♥~ My Jesus Journal Time! ~♥~

#33

God's Mercy

If I look back at my entire life, the three things that come to mind as my four greatest regrets are that I didn't know and believe in and follow the Lord Jesus Christ right from the start, that I talked about something from long ago I wish I had forgiven and let go and kept quiet about, that I did not love and honor my parents from childhood on as I should have done no matter their imperfections, and that despite going to exceeding lengths for decades to help rescue dogs I at times lost my patience in a totally unacceptable way and did not love them the way I desperately wanted to do.

God in His amazing remarkable mercy has loved and forgiven me through it all in response to my faith in Him and "godly sorrow (2 Cor. 7:10)" and repentance. How can we ever thank God sufficiently for His love and mercy? I believe we cannot. But I do believe we can show our Thanksgiving to Him and for Him in the way we choose to live our lives – by living totally surrendered to Him and His will each and every day and forevermore! Including crying out for and receiving His mercy when we need it!

"O give thanks unto the LORD; for *he is* good: because his mercy *endureth* for ever." Psalms 118:1 KJV

...

praise the Lord! ———— ∞∞ ———— hallelujah!

♥ My Jesus Journal Time! ♥

praise the Lord! ———ooo——— hallelujah!

#34

My Big Beautiful Bananas

I have been eating bananas since I was a child. I am in my 50s now, so that's a super long time. My favorite foods have changed over time, and suffice it to say peanut butter and jelly sandwiches, chocolate chip peanut butter cookies, and protein smoothies with bananas in them are some of my favorites for now anyway. So I take great delight in finding extra big bananas in the store. I enjoy them most when they ripen into a yummy sweet mush perfect for tossing in the blender I bring with me as I go from hotel to hotel in my life on the road for Jesus. You might not think finding big beautiful bananas in the store is a big deal, but it is to me. And here is why.

The reason is two-fold. First, I love them. Second, I am so extremely thankful to God for them and have spent far too much of my life not being thankful for all the "little things" with which God has blessed me. In my spoiled, take-way-too-much-for-granted years, bananas were something I wouldn't have even thought to be thankful to God for. But God has humbled me, and I realize now God's blessings range from tiny to gargantuan but all bear significance such that we should be thankful to God for each and all of them. This may not mean we stop to thank God for every single blessing small and enormous, but we should at the very least be thankful in our hearts to God – for everything with which He blesses us throughout the course of our lives!

"For the earth is the Lord's, and the fulness thereof." 1 Corinthians 10:27 KJV

...

praise the Lord! ———∞∞∞——— hallelujah!

♥ My Jesus Journal Time! ♥

#35

God's Love

God's love is so unfathomably big and beautiful that nothing on this earth could ever measure up to it which comes as no surprise because God Himself IS love! We humans tend to be so focused on what we can see, touch, feel, taste, and hear in our immediate surroundings that I am afraid we may be remiss in pouring out our hearts to God with praise and adoration in Thanksgiving for the intangible, untouchable, un-seeable, un-hearable gifts from God that truly are the most valuable gifts from God of all. This world as we know it will one day be gone, and there will be a new heavens and a new earth (2 Peter 3:13) to be enjoyed by all of God's followers. His love that never fails (1 Cor. 13:8) from which we who follow Jesus can never be separated will endure into eternity. Should we not ever thank the Lord for His endless love? Oh, yes! Forever and evermore we should thank Him!

"He that loveth not knoweth not God; for God is love." 1 John 4:8

"For I am persuaded, that neither death, nor life, nor angels, nor principalities, nor powers, nor things present, nor things to come, Nor height, nor depth, nor any other creature, shall be able to separate us from the love of God, which is in Christ Jesus our Lord." Romans 8:38-39 KJV

"And the world passeth away, and the lust thereof: but he that doeth the will of God abideth for ever." 1 John 2:17 KJV

...

praise the Lord! —————∞∞∞————— hallelujah!

My Jesus Journal Time!

#36

God's Truth

Did you know the longest Psalm in the Bible is about the Bible, God's Word? When I read Psalm 119, I am so encouraged to fall more in love not only with God but with His Word! Did you know per the Bible God's Word is Truth? Did you know Jesus is the Truth? Did you know Jesus is the "Word made flesh"? It all comes back to the Lord and the Bible, doesn't it?

Honestly, for such a long time I was totally intimidated and overwhelmed by the Bible not to mention bored, confused, and turned off. My flesh just didn't realize the utter beauty of the Bible – and that it is truly God's road map for living. I wonder in America if many of us take the Bible for granted because we are so fortunate to have easy and affordable and even free access to Bibles whereas there are places around the world where people will be killed for saying the name Jesus, for proclaiming Him as Lord, and for having a Bible and believing in God's Word.

How sorry I am for how I have taken for granted that I have 24-7 access to God through repentance and faith in the Lord Jesus Christ and to the Bible, and that even now as I write this message I have multiple print Bibles along with access to the Bible online and on my phone. Oh, let us be thankful, so very thankful, for God's awesome, amazing, wonderful Word, oh yes!

"…Thy word *is* a lamp unto my feet, and a light unto my path."
Psalms 119:105 KJV

"In the beginning was the Word, and the Word was with God, and the Word was God…And the Word was made flesh, and dwelt among us, (and we beheld his glory, the glory as of the only begotten of the Father,) full of grace and truth." John 1:1-14 KJV

"Sanctify them through thy truth: thy word is truth." John 17:17 KJV

"And I will delight myself in thy commandments, which I have loved."
Psalms 119:47 KJV

. . .

praise the Lord! —————∞∞————— hallelujah!

❤ My Jesus Journal Time! ❤

praise the Lord! ——ooo—— hallelujah!

#37

I Don't Live in the 1800s

Okay, it's obvious I don't live in the 1800s. But what you may not know is I have many a time thought I would have done better living in the 1800s because of my love for the Lord, a simple life, the strong biblical preaching back then, the real repentance and real revivals, the focus of believers in Jesus on purity and holiness, the love for God and for family, etc. But I have quickly considered the fact that back then they didn't have heat, air conditioning, and washing machines. And the temperatures were frigid to say the least – in the fiction books I have read anyway.

What does this have to do with being thankful? As much as sometimes I have dreamed of being in another time, or a different place, or had a different relationship, had a different life's story, or had different circumstances, the reality is I am thankful for the Lord's perfect will in my life, for His perfect love and provision, remembering that He always knows best. Which is why I didn't live in the 1800's.

God's will may not be what we would have chosen, but let us be thankful He truly always does know best. Always.

"Giving thanks always for all things unto God and the Father in the name of our Lord Jesus Christ;" Ephesians 5:20 KJV

...

praise the Lord! ———∞∞——— hallelujah!

♥ My Jesus Journal Time! ♥

#38

God's Protection

I sincerely believe if we looked back at our lives and could see with perfect clarity all the bad, harm, hurt, darkness, evil, accidents, troubles, losses, etc. the Lord protected us from, we would be in awe and want to thank Him forever. Does this mean we never go through hard stuff? No! Jesus makes clear we WILL go through tribulations in this life, but that His followers can rejoice that we will be with Him forever and one day be in a place with no more pain, tears, losses, tragedies, sicknesses, etc.

In the meantime, as hard as our lives may be at times, if we would only realize how much God does protect us from on this earth, I do believe we would be humbled and astounded beyond measure.

The biggest thing the Lord protects us from when we repent and believe in Jesus Christ as Lord and in His death and resurrection and truly turn our lives over to God and His ways is from His wrath and death, hell, and the lake of fire which is the final destination of those who do not turn their lives over to the Lord. Yes, God protects us from really little things, and in-between things, and the biggest thing He protects His followers from is eternal damnation and hellfire. When was the last time you stopped everything you were doing to simply and joyfully thank God for His protection?

"These things I have spoken unto you, that in me ye might have peace. In the world ye shall have tribulation: but be of good cheer; I have overcome the world." John 16:33 KJV

...

praise the Lord! ———ꝏ——— hallelujah!

♥ My Jesus Journal Time! ♥

#39

God's Kindness

Over the years, when I have thought of kindness, I have thought of the kindness to which we are called particularly in the well known verses in the book of Galatians about bearing the fruit of God's Spirit who lives inside His followers. We are called to be people of faith, love, and much else – including kindness toward others. What I never really considered to the best of my recollection anyway is God's kindness. Oh, sure, I have given quick thought to God's "lovingkindness", and I absolutely love that word which does not seem in my experience anyway to be used in modern day English outside of when someone is speaking or writing about the Bible. But what about simple kindness, which of course is born of love? Is this not a major attribute of the Lord Himself? Oh, yes it is!

This was brought to my attention when a beloved friend of mine a few times communicated with me in her Thanksgiving to God these words: "He is so kind." Oh, yes He is! Kinder than imaginable. The perfect role model for the kindness to which we are called. His kindness is perfect, overflows with love, is so gentle, so sweet, so tender, so giving, so sacrificing, so generous, so wonderful, so comforting, so merciful, and on and on. When we think about Thanksgiving, and when we aspire to be thankful on an ongoing basis, may we not leave anything out when it comes to the wondrousness and gloriousness and goodness of God. Kindness included. Oh, let us thank the Lord for His loving – kindness! Amen!

...

praise the Lord! ———♡♡♡——— hallelujah!

My Jesus Journal Time!

praise the Lord! —————ooo————— hallelujah!

#40

God's Comfort

I cross paths with people continually who need comfort. Some people have a circle of people in their lives and don't have too much interaction outside of that circle. Given my life on the road for Jesus, and my ministry work to which I am called, I am ever meeting new people. Some I meet ever so briefly. Some remain in my life for years to come. One thing is constant. Always, always, always there are people hurting, broken, lost, sad, depressed, going through unbelievable tragedies, wounded, sick, dying, suicidal, hooked on drugs, in and out of prison, homeless, hungry, poor, and on and on. Over and again I meet people who need comfort.

And I have long since learned that all the human comfort in the world doesn't come close to the awesomely amazing loving tender gentle marvelous healing and blessed comfort of "the God of all comfort" who comforts us so wonderfully and satisfyingly and abundantly that we are left with comfort enough to give unto others in need of comfort! Do you know the comfort of the Lord? Have you shared it with others in need? Are you thankful to God for it? Have you told Him? I would imagine sharing His comfort with others in need of it is a way of telling God, Thank You Lord!

"Blessed *be* God, even the Father of our Lord Jesus Christ, the Father of mercies, and the God of all comfort; Who comforteth us in all our tribulation, that we may be able to comfort them which are in any trouble, by the comfort wherewith we ourselves are comforted of God." 2 Corinthians 1:3-4 KJV

. . .

praise the Lord! ———————∞∞———————— hallelujah!

♥ My Jesus Journal Time! ♥

#41

Bye Bye Negativity

Some people are negative by nature. Some are really, really negative by nature. I am really, really, really negative by nature and pretty much always have been. So imagine my surprise and delight at realizing that overall I have become an enormously positive person. How is that possible if negativity is my nature? Because God when He forgives our sins and gives us everlasting life through our repentance and faith in Jesus Christ and in His death and resurrection and committing our lives to God and His ways transforms us day by day as we learn to live for Him and no longer for self.

God took on a very big tough project when He took me on, but He in His love and mercy and kindness and grace and by His great power has been changing me day by day and will finish the work He began in me. This is how more and more the negativity is becoming a thing of the past while more and more I am living the way God created me to live.

If you struggle with being negative sometimes, or even a lot as I have for as long as I can remember, the #1 way I have found to combat negativity is to be totally devoted to the Lord Jesus Christ, to focus on God and the Bible and His ways and His will for me, to spend time alone in His presence praying and praising Him, seeking and hearing Him, singing to Him and enjoying Him, worshiping Him and experiencing His magnificent presence, loving and serving Him with all my heart – and CHOOSING JOY AND THANKSGIVING instead of negativity and all that goes with it.

Every time you are tempted to fall into negativity, or if you have already fallen into it, turn away from it, turn to God, and choose Thanksgiving!

...

praise the Lord! ——— ∞∞ ——— hallelujah!

My Jesus Journal Time!

praise the Lord! ———— ∞ ———— hallelujah!

#42

Your Happy Place

I usually really don't like modern day newly made up lingo especially when it's all about self knowing full well Jesus calls His followers to deny self, take up our crosses, and follow Him. I usually don't pay much attention to the sayings and try as best I can to stay focused on God and His Word and His will for my life and ministry. But I couldn't help but pay attention to yet another new saying. Perhaps you have heard it. "My happy place." Or, "Your happy place". And, "Find your happy place."

Ugh. The last thing I need is to be tempted to go back to my decades of being so self-centered and so consumed with pleasing myself and finding what made me happy and indulging in sin against God that I couldn't see past myself. Isn't what we need more than anything encouragement to deny self and to follow the leading of the Lord as we learn to live according to His ways not the world's ways? Well, something interesting happened with this particular saying. And herein lies some encouragement for you who read this message.

After decades of failing to find any kind of lasting happiness, I found "my happy place." And I could not be more thankful to God for leading me to this place. This "happy place" is the Lord and abiding in Him. In essence, loving God, trusting Him, enjoying Him, experiencing Him, looking to Him, putting my hope in Him, finding peace in Him, resting in Him, rejoicing in Him, pouring out my heart to Him, praising Him, praying to Him, seeking Him, hearing Him, spending time in His presence, delighting in Him, singing to Him, being corrected by Him, being transformed by Him, being forgiven by Him, finding grace in Him, putting my expectation in Him, communing with Him, His being my first love and my Lord and King and Savior and healer and master and best friend, having an intimate forever relationship with Him, etc.

Yes, my "happy place" is the Lord and abiding in Him. And there is nothing I am more thankful for in the universe than the Lord and abiding in Him – forevermore!

…

praise the Lord! ———◦◦◦——— hallelujah!

♥ My Jesus Journal Time! ♥

#43

Chocolate Chip Pancakes

I am probably one of the few women God ever created who for years and years of my adult life could have cared less about chocolate. Then everything changed. I went through a good long period of feeling like I couldn't live without it. Chocolate this. Chocolate that. Everything chocolate. So much so any other food paled in comparison. My chocolate consumption got out of hand. So much so two friends said they would pray God would take the chocolate from my life. He did. Then after a good long while I started eating chocolate again. Moderately. Thank the Lord. I am not obsessed with it now. I simply enjoy it. It's a special treat I eat in moderation. For which I am thankful to God.

Speaking of Thanksgiving, imagine my delight and pleasure concerning this. A beautiful friend who with her husband owns a restaurant came right to my hotel room door, knocked, and lovingly delivered – for free – a thick stack of delicious chocolate chip pancakes along with a container of chocolate sauce and two more containers – filled with chocolate chips! Yum exceedingly!

If you think this message is about chocolate, it's really not. It's about recognizing that God's love and gifts and blessings and goodness are truly endless. And, for each and every one of them, chocolate chip pancakes and beautiful friends included – we should be THANKFUL! Hallelujah, YUM, Amen!

"Praise ye the LORD. O give thanks unto the LORD; for *he is* good: for his mercy [some other versions use the word/s "love" and "lovingkindness" instead of mercy] *endureth* for ever." Psalms 106:1 KJV

...

praise the Lord! ———ꝏ——— hallelujah!

♥ My Jesus Journal Time! ♥

#44

Thankful for Serving

When I came across a passage in the Bible about the apostle Paul being thankful essentially for God calling him into his ministry work, the word ministry per Strong's concordance coming from a Greek word that also is used as "service", I knew immediately there was a powerful message. About serving. About Thanksgiving. About being thankful for serving.

We humans in our sin nature without God are self-centered, selfish, self-seeking, etc. We may think of serving as an obligation. We may think of it as a way to get attention and praise and acceptance from people. We may think of it as a way to feel good about ourselves. And so on. But when we believe in Jesus Christ as Lord, and follow Jesus Christ as Lord, and when our serving is not self-centered but is about serving the Lord and serving others in His name for His glory, then we come to know the blessedness of humbling ourselves and loving and serving God with all our hearts. And we see that serving, and God calling us to serve, and God enabling us to serve, and God giving us opportunities to serve, and God giving us the resources to serve, and God giving us the opportunity to love and glorify Him in serving, this is something for which we can – and should – be indescribably THANKFUL! Thank you, God, that we get to love and serve you with every ounce of our hearts, AMEN!

"And I thank Christ Jesus our Lord, who hath enabled me, for that he counted me faithful, putting me into the ministry; Who was before a blasphemer, and a persecutor, and injurious: but I obtained mercy, because I did *it* ignorantly in unbelief. And the grace of our Lord was exceeding abundant with faith and love which is in Christ Jesus." 1 Timothy 1:12-14 KJV

...

praise the Lord! ———ᴏᴏᴏ——— hallelujah!

~♥~ My Jesus Journal Time! ~♥~

#45

More Peas Please!

When I peered into my little hotel room fridge, which I have become well accustomed to given I have been on the road for some years now full-time loving and serving the Lord and others, I saw them! I was thrilled! Wow! What a surprise! I had forgotten about them! What? The peas! Oh, yes, that very day I could eat more peas! Bring on the peas! More peas please! Perhaps you wonder what my peas in their little container could have to do with being thankful to the Lord. Please let me tell you.

Peas are yummy. Peas are healthy. Peas are easy to prepare. Peas have great fiber. Peas are affordable. Peas are perfect when you're on the road full-time and don't have a kitchen in your hotel room nor like to cook anyway. Peas are easy to deal with in the microwave. Peas do well in the fridge. Peas fit well into a little cheap dollar store container. And peas are something I once had absolutely no desire for. No interest in. No regard for. Could have cared less about. And certainly was not thankful for.

But God is teaching me day by day to be thankful for all things whether big, small, easy, hard, what I wanted or what I begged Him not to have happen, absolutely whatever it may be, oh yes, He is teaching me to be thankful in all things. And for all things. Even for peas. More peas please!

A beloved friend who has been like a spiritual Mom to me for years pointed out the following verse long ago. It's a perfect fit for my "more peas please" little testimony – and for each and every day of our lives and forever and ever, AMEN!

"Rejoice evermore. Pray without ceasing. In every thing give thanks: for this is the will of God in Christ Jesus concerning you." 1 Thessalonians 5:16-18 KJV

…

praise the Lord! ———ᴏᴏᴏ——— hallelujah!

♥ My Jesus Journal Time! ♥

praise the Lord! ———ooo——— hallelujah!

#46

Being Thankful – from the Heart!

Perhaps you know the Bible story about how Jesus multiplied a tiny amount of fish and bread so a mass number of people ended up being fed. Jesus prayed with Thanksgiving to God the Father for His miraculous provision of food. Know what strikes me? Instead of bowing down His head and closing His eyes like most people seem to do when they pray before a meal, He looked up to God in heaven and humbly thanked Him!

I wonder how much of the time we who follow Jesus do things the way other believers in Jesus do them assuming that is the one right way to do them. I grew up in a Jewish family that didn't believe in God, so much of Christianity was foreign to me until decades later. When I first really paid attention to how Jesus' followers prayed before a meal, I assumed it was mandatory that we bow our heads and close our eyes. But that is not how Jesus prayed before that miraculous meal!

What do you think our Thanksgiving to God would truly be like and look like if we let go of any traditions made by people and simply did what we believe is in line with the Bible and comes from our hearts yearning to bring God love, praise, honor, joy, pleasure, and glory? Writing this message really makes me think!

God wants us to worship Him "in spirit and in truth", and I feel compelled to encourage you as well as myself to be sincere, genuine, and true & and to be totally devoted to God in our love for and Thanksgiving to Him. Even if that means looking up to heaven to THANK THE LORD before a meal! Hallelujah!

"And when he had taken the five loaves and the two fishes, he looked up to heaven, and blessed, and brake the loaves, and gave *them* to his disciples to set before them; and the two fishes divided he among them all. And they did all eat, and were filled." Mark 6:41-42 KJV

"But the hour cometh, and now is, when the true worshippers shall worship the Father in spirit and in truth: for the Father seeketh such to worship him. God *is* a Spirit: and they that worship him must worship *him* in spirit and in truth." John 4:23-24 KJV

praise the Lord! ————∞∞————— hallelujah!

♥ My Jesus Journal Time! ♥

#47

God's Peace

The Bible shows us that blessedly by God's grace alone He is the "God of peace", and that we can have the "peace of God." There are many Bible verses about the peace we can have through faith in and our lives being devoted to the Lord Jesus Christ. There is truly no peace we can have on this earth that can compare to the peace we can have in God.

Isn't it something how much time we spend looking for peace on this earth when in fact any worldly peace such as is found in reading a good book, taking a walk by the ocean, listening to quiet music, etc. can never measure up to the peace we find in the Lord and in a forever relationship with Him. I want to encourage you to reflect on the peace you have found in the Lord, or the peace you desire to find in Him if you have not already done so, and to thank the Lord for His precious priceless peace. Thank you God!

Here are a few verses to bless and inspire you, and may the Lord get all the glory for the peace He brings to you through His Spirit, His heart, His love, His Word, and in every other way He blesses His children with His peace. Oh, be thankful! Thank the Lord for His peace and for all with which He blesses you each and every day of your life! Amen!

"Now the God of peace, that brought again from the dead our Lord Jesus, that great shepherd of the sheep, through the blood of the everlasting covenant, Make you perfect in every good work to do his will, working in you that which is wellpleasing in his sight, through Jesus Christ; to whom *be* glory for ever and ever. Amen." Hebrews 13:20-21 KJV

"And let the peace of God rule in your hearts, to the which also ye are called in one body; and be ye thankful." Colossians 3:15 KJV

"Thou wilt keep *him* in perfect peace, *whose* mind *is* stayed *on thee:* because he trusteth in thee." Isaiah 26:3

There are so very many more verses in the Bible about peace! So hoping you will be inspired to go look for them and enjoy them! Enjoy His peace! And be thankful!

...

praise the Lord! ———ᴏᴏᴏ——— hallelujah!

♥ My Jesus Journal Time! ♥

praise the Lord! ——ooo—— hallelujah!

#48

Peace with God

It would be hard to imagine there has ever been a human who walked the face of this earth who did not want peace and in some way pursue it. Thank the Lord He is the God of peace and that we can have the peace of God – and that we can have peace WITH God. I never noticed the marvelous intricacies of peace concerning God until I read a book long ago by evangelist Billy Graham who has since gone on to be with the Lord. The Lord used his writing to help me to go deeper in my understanding of peace. Including when it comes to peace WITH God. How can we have peace WITH God?

We are all sinners separated from God. But God in His amazing love for His Creation sent His only Son Jesus to the earth to live a perfect life, to the cross to die an unimaginable death to pay the sin penalty we deserve, and to raise Him from the dead. So all who turn from our sins, believe in Jesus Christ as Lord and in His death and resurrection, truly turning our lives over to God and His ways, are forgiven, HAVE "PEACE WITH GOD", are promised forever life with Him, and the Holy Spirit comes to live in us. Peace WITH God comes from God through Jesus' death and resurrection and our repentance and faith in Jesus and our lives being surrendered to Him.

We CANNOT have peace with God as sinners who refuse to repent and reject Christ as Lord. But we CAN have peace beyond imagination now and forever when we genuinely commit our lives to Christ now and forevermore! Oh, how can we ever thank God enough for His love and mercy and salvation – and PEACE? Let us praise Him forevermore!

"Therefore being justified by faith, we have peace with God through our Lord Jesus Christ: By whom also we have access by faith into this grace wherein we stand, and rejoice in hope of the glory of God." Romans 5:1-2 KJV

…

praise the Lord! ———ᴑᴑᴑ——— hallelujah!

♥ My Jesus Journal Time! ♥

#49

Thanksgiving for Trials & Tribulations

How can God's children have Thanksgiving to Him when we're in the thick of our trials? We can turn to the Lord & put our trust in Him & rejoice IN HIM & be thankful TO HIM for His love, beauty, magnificence, splendor, glory, comfort, healing, hope, peace, joy, wisdom, promise of eternity to His followers, kindness, blessings, provision, mercy, lordship, sovereignty, His Spirit, His Word, for how He transforms us through our trials, for how He draws us closer to Himself, for how He uses our trials to prepare us for eternity with Him & to better equip us to love & help others, for intimacy with Him, and on & on go the reasons we can rejoice & be thankful even in our hardest times!

May these verses be an encouragement to you – to be thankful to God even in the hardest of times in your life!

"And not only *so,* but we glory in tribulations also: knowing that tribulation worketh patience; And patience, experience; and experience, hope: And hope maketh not ashamed; because the love of God is shed abroad in our hearts by the Holy Ghost which is given unto us." Romans 5:3-5 KJV

"My brethren, count it all joy when ye fall into divers temptations; Knowing *this,* that the trying of your faith worketh patience. But let patience have *her* perfect work, that ye may be perfect and entire, wanting nothing."
James 1:2-4 KJV

"Beloved, think it not strange concerning the fiery trial which is to try you, as though some strange thing happened unto you: But rejoice, inasmuch as ye are partakers of Christ's sufferings; that, when his glory shall be revealed, ye may be glad also with exceeding joy." 1 Peter 4:12-13 KJV

"Wherein ye greatly rejoice, though now for a season, if need be, ye are in heaviness through manifold temptations: That the trial of your faith, being much more precious than of gold that perisheth, though it be tried with fire, might be found unto praise and honour and glory at the appearing of Jesus Christ:" 1 Peter 1:6-7 KJV

praise the Lord! ———ooo——— hallelujah!

My Jesus Journal Time!

#50

Thank God for Rejection

If there is anything I hate I have tons of experience with, it's rejection. Ick. Yuck. Ugh. I despise it. I have always been sensitive and emotional. You can only imagine. Yet not only has the Lord been teaching me to handle it with trust in Him and love, grace, mercy, and forgiveness for those who reject me, but I have learned to be thankful for it. How so?

God has used it to draw me ever closer to Himself and to deepen my relationship with Him, to refine me, grow me, teach me, test me, purify me, and cleanse me, and to be more sensitive, compassionate, kind, loving, merciful, and forgiving toward others including those who go through their own rejection as well as toward those who reject me. Sometimes I am rejected by people He wants to protect me from and who are not part of His perfect will for my life. I am thankful to the Lord for all the good He brings through rejection in spite of how yucky it still feels.

I have faced rejection for many reasons over the years including as a result of proclaiming Jesus Christ as Lord and living for the Lord according to His ways.

What I am most thankful for concerning rejection is how to combat it. By turning to the Lord and His Word, by receiving and experiencing God's love, and by showing and sharing His love and forgiveness with others. Ultimate answer? God and His love!

When facing rejection, I encourage you to turn to the Lord and to the Bible!

Here is some encouragement, but the Bible is filled with tons and tons more!

"Yea, and all that will live godly in Christ Jesus shall suffer persecution." 2 Timothy 3:12 KJV

"Blessed are ye, when men shall hate you, and when they shall separate you *from their company,* and shall reproach *you,* and cast out your name as evil, for the Son of man's sake. Rejoice ye in that day, and leap for joy: for, behold, your reward *is* great in heaven: for in the like manner did their fathers unto the prophets." Luke 6:22-23 KJV

"And we have known and believed the love that God hath to us. God is love; and he that dwelleth in love dwelleth in God, and God in him." 1 John 4:16 KJV

praise the Lord! ———•○○○•——— hallelujah!

♥ My Jesus Journal Time! ♥

#51

Don't Feel Like Being Thankful?

Sometimes I'm simply not in the mood for being thankful. I am irritable. Tired. Exhausted. Cranky. People are driving me crazy. I'm feeling impatient. Being impatient. I'm having a bad day. Too many challenges. God didn't answer my begging Him for something I desperately wanted. I just went through another big loss. Whatever the reason, I have absolutely no desire to be thankful. In the past, I know exactly what I would have done. I would have been unthankful to God, unthankful to others, and made sure the whole wide world had the opportunity to come to my pity party. Things are different now. Very different.

I now see Thanksgiving as a choice. As a decision to make. I can choose to be thankful to the Lord – or not. And considering God is worthy of all praise, honor, glory – and Thanksgiving – now and forever, I believe the right, God-revering, God-fearing, God-loving thing to do is to be thankful to the Lord no matter how I feel.

I believe the best place to start when we're feeling unthankful is to turn away from any and all sin, to purge it from our hearts, words, and actions, to seek and receive His forgiveness, and to start with a clean heart! A heart filled with humility, love for, devotion to, and Thanksgiving to the Lord most high!

"And every man that hath this hope in him purifieth himself, even as he is pure." 1 John 3:3 KJV

"Having therefore these promises, dearly beloved, let us cleanse ourselves from all filthiness of the flesh and spirit, perfecting holiness in the fear of God." 2 Corinthians 7:1 KJV

...

praise the Lord! —————ooo————— hallelujah!

♥ My Jesus Journal Time! ♥

#52

God's Chastening

One of the last things in the world I ever thought I would be thankful for is God's chastening, His correction, His conviction, and His leading me to repentance. But I was reminded no more than a minute or two ago of how thankful I am for all this. What just happened? The Lord just chastened me for some impulsive and selfish behavior. I had contacted a friend and told her something to get a burden off my shoulders. But I hadn't considered she had a huge burden on her shoulders already and didn't need a call from me let alone a call about some difficult stuff going on in the world. I had been wrong. And God, in His love for me as His child and servant, has brought the necessary correction.

Why was I thankful for God chastening me and leading me to repentance, and why should we all be thankful for this? The verses below say it all.

"And ye have forgotten the exhortation which speaketh unto you as unto children, My son, despise not thou the chastening of the Lord, nor faint when thou art rebuked of him: For whom the Lord loveth he chasteneth, and scourgeth every son whom he receiveth. If ye endure chastening, God dealeth with you as with sons; for what son is he whom the father chasteneth not? But if ye be without chastisement, whereof all are partakers, then are ye bastards, and not sons. Furthermore we have had fathers of our flesh which corrected *us,* and we gave *them* reverence: shall we not much rather be in subjection unto the Father of spirits, and live? For they verily for a few days chastened *us* after their own pleasure; but he for *our* profit, that *we* might be partakers of his holiness. Now no chastening for the present seemeth to be joyous, but grievous: nevertheless afterward it yieldeth the peaceable fruit of righteousness unto them which are exercised thereby."
Hebrews 12:5-11 KJV

...

praise the Lord! ———— ∞∞ ———— hallelujah!

♥ My Jesus Journal Time! ♥

#53

So Many Blessings

I was friends with a woman many years ago whom if I recall correctly had as part of her email address the words "so many blessings." Now I honestly don't know where she stood with the Lord and if she was a born again follower of His, and I at the time was a believer in the Lord but most assuredly not a totally devoted follower. But this message isn't about where our faith in the Lord did or didn't stand all those years ago. Nor is it about "so many blessings". It's about the fact God's blessings are infinite! And how we should strive day in and day out to be thankful for ALL our blessings from God and to thank Him – and BLESS Him - for them!

"But we will bless the LORD from this time forth and for evermore. Praise the LORD." Psalms 115:18 KJV

…

praise the Lord! ———∞∞— hallelujah!

♥ My Jesus Journal Time! ♥

#54

Thankful for Thanksgiving

The very most important aspect of Thanksgiving to God is that God be praised and thanked for His amazingness and awesomeness and wonderfulness and wondrousness and gloriousness, but there is something else that happens when we express to God our thankfulness in my experience anyway. There is such great joy in my heart, such passionate rejoicing, such great love and adoration I feel, such a feeling of blessedness when I take the time to thank the Lord! Might sound funny, but it's true. I am thankful for Thanksgiving to the Lord. Are you? Try praising the Lord and see what happens! Praise Him for the purpose of thanking and blessing Him, not for selfish gain. But watch what happens in your heart and countenance when you praise, praise, praise the Lord in Thanksgiving and with great, great love for Him!

"Praise ye the LORD. Praise God in his sanctuary: praise him in the firmament of his power. Praise him for his mighty acts: praise him according to his excellent greatness. Praise him with the sound of the trumpet: praise him with the psaltery and harp. Praise him with the timbrel and dance: praise him with stringed instruments and organs. Praise him upon the loud cymbals: praise him upon the high sounding cymbals. Let every thing that hath breath praise the LORD. Praise ye the LORD." Psalms 150:1-6 KJV

...

praise the Lord! ——•∞∞•—— hallelujah!

♥ My Jesus Journal Time! ♥

#55

Intimacy with Jesus

Some people love and crave relationships with others. They yearn for intimacy with people. They hunger and thirst for intensely close relationships. They want to know and be known deeply by another or others. I have always been this way. I love, love, love intimacy. But it never crossed my mind in all my years of chasing after men, and relationships with them, and friends, and friendships with them, and whole groups of people and strong bonds with them that the intimate and only perfectly satisfying relationship in our lives God created us to have above all else is with Him! And that when we have that, everything else no matter how wonderful it may be pales in comparison!

Now that I have an amazingly rich, vibrant, ever growing, ever deepening relationship with the Lord, and now that I spend time with Him daily alone in His presence loving and praising and worshiping Him, singing to Him, praying to Him and seeking Him, reading the Bible, hearing Him and responding to Him, pouring out my heart to Him, learning to trust and rest in Him, all of which to me is a part of learning to abide in Christ, I have come to see there is no greater, no more fulfilling, no more satisfying, no more rewarding intimacy we can have with anyone than the intimate relationship God desires for us to have with Him!

I could not be more thankful to God for my relationship with Him, and I want to encourage you to pursue the Lord and an ever growing relationship with Him and His will for your life more than you pursue anything or anyone else. And BE THANKFUL to God for God and for your relationship with Him, oh yes!

"I *am* my beloved's, and my beloved *is* mine: he feedeth among the lilies." Song of Solomon 6:3 KJV

...

praise the Lord! ———∘∘∘——— hallelujah!

♥ My Jesus Journal Time! ♥

praise the Lord! ——ooo—— hallelujah!

#56

Thankful for God's Warnings!

Children aren't always thrilled when they hurry off to run across the street to go play with their friends only to have their parents warn them about the traffic, tell them to stop and look both ways, and not cross until they are safe to do so. Oh, sure, they may be thankful afterward. But before? Not altogether likely! Nor are we adults always so thankful – as we should be – when God warns us to not do something. He warns us because He is Lord, King, Savior, and Creator, in His love for us, because His will for us is best, because He wants us to obey Him not rebel against Him, because He wants to bless us not chasten us, because He wants to save us from the consequences of temptation and sin, because He wants to protect us from something or someone, and because He wants us to end up in heaven not hell and the lake of fire, etc.

Sadly sometimes whether or not we obey God we are like children all hurt and upset and complaining when God warns us not to do something. What we should be 100% of the time in response to God's warnings is humble, obedient, and THANKFUL!

We would do well to get rid of our pity and complaining and choose to be thankful to the Lord for warning us. Don't you think?

"But with many of them God was not well pleased: for they were overthrown in the wilderness. Now these things were our examples, to the intent we should not lust after evil things, as they also lusted. Neither be ye idolaters, as *were* some of them; as it is written, The people sat down to eat and drink, and rose up to play. Neither let us commit fornication, as some of them committed, and fell in one day three and twenty thousand. Neither let us tempt Christ, as some of them also tempted, and were destroyed of serpents. Neither murmur ye, as some of them also murmured, and were destroyed of the destroyer. Now all these things happened unto them for ensamples: and they are written for our admonition [original Greek word per Strong's concordance also translated whereby "warning" is mentioned], upon whom the ends of the world are come." 1 Cor. 10:5-11 KJV

praise the Lord! ———∞∞∞——— hallelujah!

♥ My Jesus Journal Time! ♥

#57

Thank God for New Vision!

Praise the Lord, as I write this, I am wearing my new prescription reading glasses. I love them. I tried prescription reading glasses once before but had a bad experience with the company and ended up with glasses that ended up causing more trouble than good. My vision has gone downhill as I have aged, and I am sad to say I didn't realize how bad things had gotten until I was editing a book I had written and realized my blurry vision was making was making writing and editing pretty hard. Still, it was a long while until I finally surrendered and went to Walmart to get a vision test and order glasses. I am so thankful to the Lord for providing my glasses and for the help He sent me and for the money to get them. But the good new and clear vision I now have when I wear my glasses is nothing when compared with the "good new and clear vision" God has given me in life. And for this I am exceedingly thankful to the Lord!

Can you relate to any of this? God has given me the "good new and clear vision" to see my sin, to realize my need to repent and be forgiven, to see and know and receive His love, to see and appreciate His majesty and splendor and beauty, to see and appreciate His grace and mercy and kindness and care and compassion and goodness and wisdom, to see where I need to grow, to see how nothing I am without Him, to see when I need to purify myself, to see my continual need for Him, to see His blessedness and blessings, to see His goodness and to acknowledge and praise Him for it, to read the Bible and learn to live by it, to see others' needs and how He wants me to love and serve them, and on and on. He has most assuredly given me new vision!

When we repent and receive Jesus Christ as Lord, truly surrendering our lives to God, He makes us "new creatures". And, as new creatures, we are given new vision, don't you think? The ability to see what we couldn't see before. And with this comes an amazing opportunity to tell and show the Lord how very thankful we are!

"Therefore if any man *be* in Christ, *he is* a new creature: old things are passed away; behold, all things are become new." 2 Corinthians 5:17

praise the Lord! ———ooo——— hallelujah!

♥ My Jesus Journal Time! ♥

#58

Thank You God for Saying No

Dear God, thank you for every single time in my life you have ever answered my prayers with a big, "NO." Father, I am so sorry that I have so lacked trust in you, that I have had such a self-pitying, angry, hurt, bitter, etc. response to you when you have refused to give me what I prayed for. Lord, you always know what's best. And I have pridefully exalted myself and felt my will was best. Lord, I am so sorry! And I want to take this opportunity to say THANK YOU for every time you have in fact refused me what I asked for from you. God, I wish I could promise to do a better job in the future. But I fall so very far short. So I simply ask you now, dear Lord, to help me be humble, to help me think right and do right, to help me grow in trusting you, and to help me be thankful not whining and complaining when I don't get my way. God, I love you more than imaginable, and I thank you for receiving this prayer from me, dear God. Now I ask you to help every person who reads this prayer and message dear God and myself also to trust you, to pray to you, and to be humble and loving and thankful no matter how you respond to our prayers. Amen!

I didn't expect to write a prayer to begin this message. But that's exactly what poured out of my heart. And I believe there is little to say more than the prayer I have written. I believe we all could do a better job, me more so than others more than likely, with being thankful when God doesn't answer our prayers the way we so desperately want Him to. Let us grow in our love for Him, our trust in Him, our humility before Him, and our Thanksgiving to Him. Please join me in this! Let us yield ourselves to God so He can grow us in all of this! Amen!

"Trust in the LORD with all thine heart; and lean not unto thine own understanding. In all thy ways acknowledge him, and he shall direct thy paths." Proverbs 3:5-6 KJV

...

praise the Lord! ——————○○○—————— hallelujah!

♥ My Jesus Journal Time! ♥

praise the Lord! ———ooo——— hallelujah!

#59

Your Memorial Stones

In response to God's command to him, Joshua told the Israelites to gather up so-called "memorial stones" so the Israelites and future generations would remember the miracle God performed for them concerning the Jordan river. Beautiful, but also tragic. Beautiful to have a memorial to commemorate God's immeasurable goodness and to remind us to be ever thankful to Him. But also tragic that we don't continually remember on our own all of His blessedness and blessings, continually praise and thank Him for all He has done and is doing and will do, and continually tell others including future generations of His awesomeness.

Do you have any "memorial stones" in your life? Photographs? A journal? Video? Scrapbooks? Stones you paint upon each one signifying a blessing God has given you? A charm bracelet with little hearts celebrating every child and grandchild God has given you? A really good memory? A true dedication to meditating on His goodness and thanking Him continually for it? However the Lord may lead you, may you be truly committed to thinking about God's goodness and to offering Him ongoing Thanksgiving! And may you tell others on a regular basis of God's wonderfulness!

"And Joshua said unto them, Pass over before the ark of the LORD your God into the midst of Jordan, and take ye up every man of you a stone upon his shoulder, according unto the number of the tribes of the children of Israel: That this may be a sign among you, *that* when your children ask *their fathers* in time to come, saying, What *mean* ye by these stones? Then ye shall answer them, That the waters of Jordan were cut off before the ark of the covenant of the LORD; when it passed over Jordan, the waters of Jordan were cut off: and these stones shall be for a memorial unto the children of Israel for ever." Joshua 4:5-7 KJV

...

praise the Lord! ———∞∞——— hallelujah!

♥ My Jesus Journal Time! ♥

#60

Pursuing Positivity

As though there aren't already enough words and expressions in the English language, it seems like people are ever coming up with new ones. Take, for example, the word "positivity". Merriam-Dictionary online includes in its definition of positivity, "the quality or state of being positive". Though I don't recall ever hearing the word "positivity" used in relation to the Lord, I can't think of a better way to pursue and practice positivity than to make Thanksgiving to God and praise, adoration, and worship of Him a fundamental part of our everyday lives. Now that's positivity, isn't it?

When we focus on the Lord, and on His character, and His attributes, as well as His works, along with His goodness in our lives, on everything from how He created the world to what He shows us in the Bible He has planned for the new heavens and the new earth, and on and on, how can we not be positive?

I would imagine many people seeking positivity in their lives are looking in this world for something or someone to make them think positively, feel positive, and act in a positive manner. Oh, sure, they may find bits and pieces of "positivity". But let us look to the Lord, and to His Word, and thank and praise Him for all the ways in which He blesses us with "positivity" in our hearts and lives!

"Lay not up for yourselves treasures upon earth, where moth and rust doth corrupt, and where thieves break through and steal: But lay up for yourselves treasures in heaven, where neither moth nor rust doth corrupt, and where thieves do not break through nor steal: For where your treasure is, there will your heart be also." Matthew 6:19-21 KJV

May the Lord and the Bible and His promises and blessings and most of all His love and the promise to His followers of everlasting life with Him be the greatest positivity in our hearts and lives – and our #1 reason for Thanksgiving! May we be thankful for Him and to Him above all and everyone else, Hallelujah! Pursuing positivity? Craving it? Need it? Want it? Turn to the Lord – and be thankful!

…

praise the Lord! ———•ꝏ•——— hallelujah!

♥ My Jesus Journal Time! ♥

#61

Thank God for Good Fruit!

God shows us in the Bible the bad fruit we bear when we in our sinfulness live according to the flesh. He also shows us the good fruit we bear when we live in a godly manner according to His Holy Spirit who lives inside His followers. When we abide in Jesus, when we trust in the Lord, rest in Him, look to Him, put our hope in Him, have our faith in Him, seek Him, pray to Him, spend time alone with Him, read and live by His Word, hear and obey Him, follow Him, are devoted to Him, experience Him, enjoy Him, praise Him, worship Him, adore Him, sing to Him, are filled with and led by His Spirit, etc., we bear the fruit of His Spirit rather than the fruit of our sinful flesh. Let us thank the Lord for giving us the joy, honor, privilege, and blessing of bearing fruit by Him, through Him, and for Him. And let us praise Him that the fruit we bear blesses others also!

"Now the works of the flesh are manifest, which are *these;* Adultery, fornication, uncleanness, lasciviousness, Idolatry, witchcraft, hatred, variance, emulations, wrath, strife, seditions, heresies, Envyings, murders, drunkenness, revellings, and such like: of the which I tell you before, as I have also told *you* in time past, that they which do such things shall not inherit the kingdom of God. But the fruit of the Spirit is love, joy, peace, longsuffering, gentleness, goodness, faith, Meekness, temperance: against such there is no law. And they that are Christ's have crucified the flesh with the affections and lusts. If we live in the Spirit, let us also walk in the Spirit." Galatians 5:19-25 KJV

"I am the true vine, and my Father is the husbandman. Every branch in me that beareth not fruit he taketh away: and every *branch* that beareth fruit, he purgeth it, that it may bring forth more fruit. Now ye are clean through the word which I have spoken unto you. Abide in me, and I in you. As the branch cannot bear fruit of itself, except it abide in the vine; no more can ye, except ye abide in me. I am the vine, ye *are* the branches: He that abideth in me, and I in him, the same bringeth forth much fruit: for without me ye can do nothing. If a man abide not in me, he is cast forth as a branch, and is withered; and men gather them, and cast *them* into the fire, and they are burned." John 15:1-6 KJV

praise the Lord! ⎯⎯⎯♡♡♡⎯⎯⎯ hallelujah!

♥ My Jesus Journal Time! ♥

#62

People Are Listening

People listen. People hear. People pay attention. People notice. People think about. People remember. People consider what they hear others say. People are influenced by others' words. When people listen to the words of Jesus' followers, what do they hear? When people listen to what you speak, what stands out to them? Can they tell by your words that you are a follower of the Lord Jesus Christ? Can they tell you love the Lord? Do they hear that you are totally devoted to God? Or do they listen to you and hear someone who sounds like a world filled with people whose backs are turned to God?

Can they tell by your words that you're on fire for Jesus? Do they know by your words how thankful you are to God? Are your words filled with love for God and Thanksgiving to Him? Are you a godly influence on people in your actions and attitude – and in your words? Or do you have some work to do in this area of your life? People are listening. When they listen to you and me, may they hear people totally devoted to the Lord Jesus Christ who are thankful, so thankful, for the Lord and to the Lord, AMEN!

"My mouth shall speak the praise of the LORD: and let all flesh bless his holy name for ever and ever." Psalms 145:21

...

praise the Lord! ⸺ ᴼᴼᴼ ⸺ hallelujah!

❤ My Jesus Journal Time! ❤

praise the Lord! ——ooo—— hallelujah!

#63

Looking Back with Thanksgiving

Three times so far as of the writing of this book in my years thus far on the road full-time for Jesus and ministry full-time with my special needs ministry dogs, the Lord has sent me to New York City for seasons of ministry work there. I doubt I will ever forget the time He made clear He wanted me to stay through the coldest stretch of a New York City winter. I have become so sensitive to cold that I can get goose bumps at 70 degrees. Imagine my shock, dismay, and fear when God made clear His will to me.

When it comes to Thanksgiving, I believe we should be thankful to the Lord for all of His blessings in the present AND for all He has done in the past. We should be able to look back at different seasons of our lives and remember and rejoice over and praise and thank the Lord for all He did in various seasons.

I had prayed that winter the Lord would give New York City the mildest winter it had ever had in the history of the city. It may not have been the very mildest, but that winter was assuredly unbelievably mild in temperature. I had prayed for really good heat in my apartment as the heat in New York City apartments is often free but controlled by the landlords. My heat was so hot I thought one of my dogs might overheat. The temperature read 88 degrees one time! Others had prayed for my safety. God kept me safe in a dangerous city and through some dangerous situations. Oh, the list goes on. This was several years ago, but still I remember God's blessedness in that season of my life. And still, I am so very thankful to Him!

I encourage you to keep your heart filled with memories of God's goodness in the past. And may you continually thank Him for what He has done and is doing and will do throughout the course of your life! Most of all, may you thank Him that He is Lord and for all the amazing aspects and attributes and wondrousness of Jesus Christ being Lord forever and ever, AMEN!

...

praise the Lord! ———ooo——— hallelujah!

♥ My Jesus Journal Time! ♥

#64

Be An Inspiration!

I have had people in my life who have been such an inspiration to me for a variety of reasons! Those who have been the greatest inspiration to me are those who have loved and followed the Lord with all their hearts and who have been humbly and boldly and wonderfully thankful to Him!

Do you want to be a great inspiration to others? I can't think of a better way than to turn from your sins, believe in Jesus Christ as Lord and in His death and resurrection, be totally devoted to God and His ways, receive His forgiveness and the promise of forever life with Him, be filled with and led by His Holy Spirit, live utterly for Him and no longer for yourself, love and serve Him with all your heart and tell the world about Him, and don't ever hold back your Thanksgiving to Him! Be thankful to God with every ounce of your heart! And as you bless Him with your thankfulness, show and tell the world how thankful you are to God! What an inspiration you will be! Oh, praise the Lord! Glory be to the Lord, AMEN!

"And let them sacrifice the sacrifices of thanksgiving, and declare his works with rejoicing." Psalms 107:22 KJV

...

praise the Lord! ———•ᴼᴼᴼ•——— hallelujah!

♥ My Jesus Journal Time! ♥

#65

Exhausted But Thankful

I am exhausted as I write this. I have only been writing this book for just a few days, but I am already by God's grace more than half way through. Miraculous, I know. All glory to God for this. Mind you, I could really use some very good sleep. But instead of good sleep, for the past few nights I have had trouble staying asleep. Which is pretty typical for me. But when the Lord nudged me to get out of bed and start writing again – in the middle of the night – imagine how my flesh felt. Sleepy! So sleepy! No way! Why can't I just go back to sleep? I knew what to do. I submitted to God, got up, had already prayed some, prayed a little more, heated up some hot cereal for a snack, and headed for my computer to write. Exhausted. But so thankful.

Usually when I'm exhausted the last thing in the world I feel like being is thankful. But God has been teaching me to be thankful at all times. No matter what. No matter my circumstances. No matter whether I'm wide awake or totally exhausted. There is never a justification for not being thankful to God.

So here I am. Still exhausted. But so thankful. To God. Forever thankful.

Are you thankful? What if you were to be thankful to God all the time? No matter what. Unconditionally. Oh, may it be so. Amen!

"I will bless the LORD at all times: his praise *shall* continually *be* in my mouth." Psalms 34:1

...

praise the Lord! ——ooo—— hallelujah!

♥ My Jesus Journal Time! ♥

#66

God Hears My Cries!

I was singing joyfully to the Lord in my usual fashion of making up little songs to sing to Him when I heard myself essentially singing to Him how thankful I was for how He hears my cries. I am not in any way gifted in song, but those words that poured forth from my heart and mouth were so powerful to me. So true. So worth repeating. So worth sharing with you.

Please think about it. The Creator of the universe, Lord of Lords, King of Kings, God almighty, He hears the cries of His people. He hears us when we pour out our hearts to Him. He hears us when we cry out to Him with hurt, with grief, with desperation, with pleas for wisdom and direction, with yearning for more of His love and fellowship, with thirst for help living righteously, with hunger for holiness, with deep desire for mercy and forgiveness, with great need for provision, with standing in the gap as we pray for others in dire need, with prayers for people all around the world, etc. Oh, yes, He hears the cries of His people! Oh, how wonderful is the Lord! Oh, should not we not thank Him and thank Him and thank Him for hearing the cries of His followers? Most assuredly, YES!

"In my distress I called upon the LORD, and cried unto my God: he heard my voice out of his temple, and my cry came before him, *even* into his ears." Psalms 18:6 KJV

"I waited patiently for the LORD; and he inclined unto me, and heard my cry." Psalms 40:1 KJV

"Nevertheless he regarded their affliction, when he heard their cry:" Psalms 106:44 KJV

...

praise the Lord! ———∞∞——— hallelujah!

♥ My Jesus Journal Time! ♥

praise the Lord! ——————ooo—————— hallelujah!

#67

Thanksgiving Day

For many years I LOVED the Thanksgiving Day holiday. I LOVED the family gathering round, family friends coming over, family traditions, all the fabulous food, the men watching football, the girls watching soap operas (I didn't believe in God back then and would never watch one again now that I love Him and live for Him!), taking walks in the cool autumn weather, laughing, playing, crying when a young man I professed to love didn't come for Thanksgiving, eating and eating, then eating some more, listening to my Dad given the annual Thanksgiving toast (my Jewish family didn't believe in God so we didn't thank Him!), etc. Then for many years I HATED Thanksgiving and all holidays. Long story short, I was kicked out of my family for talking about something really hard that happened a long time ago. Though God has mercifully brought some family members back into my life, I am still not allowed to go "home" for holidays. Thanksgiving became such an exceedingly painful day of the year for me.

Today, as I write this, is Thanksgiving Day. I am not with the family I adore. My parents are seniors now. I don't know how many more Thanksgivings my family will gather for the Thanksgiving Day holiday. None of them so far have turned their lives over to the Lord. I love them dearly and pray desperately to God to save them and give them everlasting life with Him.

So perhaps you assume I am miserable today. Actually, I am overflowing with love, peace, hope, and joy. Today is just another day of Thanksgiving to me. It is no different than any other. It is a day as all days are to be thankful to God that He is God, that He has given me forever life with Him, that I have an everlasting relationship with Him, and for the countless blessings He has bestowed upon me throughout my life. And I am so thankful He has given me exceeding love and mercy for my family, and I thank Him for hearing my cries to Him for their salvation.

May every day in our lives be a day of Thanksgiving to the Lord!

...

praise the Lord! ———·ᵕᵕᵕ·——— hallelujah!

♥ My Jesus Journal Time! ♥

#68

So Thankful for JOY!

For years I was a miserable woman. I was filled with hurt, sorrow, grief, bitterness, complaining, self-pity, negativity etc., and this was all coupled with loads of drama and trying to drag everyone into my troubles. Every once in a while I would have a few sprinkles of joy on top of my mountain of misery, but the joy was fleeting. If it's possible to be addicted to misery, I think I was. Now mind you I have had tons of really hard stuff in my life. But I have since learned that joy is possible and promised no matter what we go through in life WHEN WE ARE FOLLOWERS OF THE LORD JESUS CHRIST AND LIVE THE WAY WE ARE CALLED TO LIVE. HUMBLY AND LOVINGLY AND REVERENTLY AND DEVOTEDLY SURRENDERED TO GOD!

I am one of those people whose life story is such that I struggle with one thing or another on a daily basis. But no matter how my days are now, whether relatively easy or extraordinarily hard or somewhere in between, I now have a clear understanding that JOY is promised me by God and that I have access to it 24-7. I am not promised to always have joy in my life's circumstances and the world around me, but I can have it every breath I take by finding joy IN THE LORD JESUS CHRIST AND IN A FOREVER RELATIONSHIP WITH THE LORD! Today I don't just have joy. I overflow with it whereby those around me get to see it and be drawn to God through it. This is the JOY OF JESUS, and I could not be more thankful for "THE JOY OF THE LORD." Got joy?

In my experience, the #1 way to EN-JOY the JOY OF GOD is to spend time alone in His presence and reading and meditating on the Bible – loving, adoring, praising, worshiping, singing to, praying to, seeking, hearing, obeying, experiencing, enjoying, growing in, being transformed by, communing with, having intimate fellowship WITH THE LORD! Be thankful for the joy of Jesus!

"… for the joy of the LORD is your strength." Nehemiah 8:10 KJV

"Be glad in the LORD, and rejoice, ye righteous: and shout for joy, all *ye that are* upright in heart." Psalms 32:11 KJV praise the Lord! ———●●●——— hallelujah!

My Jesus Journal Time!

#69

Celebrating Victories

So many times in the Old Testament people celebrated victories and thanked the Lord with great rejoicing when the Lord delivered them from their enemies. The Old Testament is filled with so many battles, but it is also filled with so much praising the Lord. When the people yielded themselves to the Lord and lived in obedience to Him, He delivered them time and time again. Story after story in the Bible, the people knew to give God the glory. They knew to give the Lord the praise.

When you and I look at our own lives, how good are we at giving God all the glory and thanking Him for the victories in life He gives us? Do we celebrate and rejoice and praise Him and tell others what awesome works God has done in our lives? Or do we give the credit to ourselves and to others and hold back the glory from God who is worthy of all honor, glory, and praise?

I want to encourage you to reflect on the past and to consider the present and to be careful in the future to remember to THANK THE LORD for all the ways in which He delivers you and sets you free and gives you victories throughout your life. To the Lord be ALL the glory!

"For I will not trust in my bow, neither shall my sword save me. But thou hast saved us from our enemies, and hast put them to shame that hated us. In God we boast all the day long, and praise thy name for ever. Selah." Psalms 44:6-8 KJV

"The LORD liveth; and blessed *be* my rock; and exalted be the God of the rock of my salvation. It *is* God that avengeth me, and that bringeth down the people under me, And that bringeth me forth from mine enemies: thou also hast lifted me up on high above them that rose up against me: thou hast delivered me from the violent man. Therefore I will give thanks unto thee, O LORD, among the heathen, and I will sing praises unto thy name." 2 Samuel 22:47-50 KJV

...

praise the Lord! ——————◦◦◦—————— hallelujah!

♥ My Jesus Journal Time! ♥

#70

Our Weakness, God's Strength

I once wrote a devotional message called "The Weakest Woman in the World". I was referring to myself of course. Sure there are probably lots of weak people around the world. But I am so incredibly, incredibly weak in so many ways. The wonderful news is God's strength is perfected in what? Our weakness! I am so thrilled, and so over-the-top thankful to the Lord, for HIS STRENGTH which is such a huge, huge part of my life every single day. I believe with all my heart the best thing we can do, which goes against what the world teaches us, is to humble ourselves and confess our weakness and look to the Lord for His strength. And to not take credit for the strength in us but to GIVE THE LORD THE GLORY for HIS STRENGTH.

I absolutely love how the apostle Paul writes of "boasting" in his weaknesses. The world sure doesn't teach us to do that, does it? We're taught to hide our weaknesses and to pretend to be strong, aren't we? Well, I am inspired by Paul and have no trouble now telling the world, I AM WEAK. Oh, God is so infinitely strong! Praise the Lord for HIS STRENGTH.

Here are some verses I believe will encourage you! Thank the Lord for His strength! Glory be to God! I encourage you to study the word "strength" in the Bible. I find such hope and strength in the Bible – including in the many verses about strength!

"And lest I should be exalted above measure through the abundance of the revelations, there was given to me a thorn in the flesh, the messenger of Satan to buffet me, lest I should be exalted above measure. For this thing I besought the Lord thrice, that it might depart from me. And he said unto me, My grace is sufficient for thee: for my strength is made perfect in weakness. Most gladly therefore will I rather glory [also "boast" per Strong's concordance] in my infirmities [also "weakness" per Strong's concordance], that the power of Christ may rest upon me." 2 Corinthians 12:7-9 KJV

"Seek the LORD, and his strength: seek his face evermore." Psalms 105:4 KJV

…

praise the Lord! ———ooo——— hallelujah!

♥ My Jesus Journal Time! ♥

#71

Contagious Thanksgiving

Usually when I hear or think about the word "contagious", it's in the context of sickness. The flu is contagious. That cold is contagious. Is that virus contagious? But the word contagious doesn't have to be associated only with illness! When I think of contagious, I think of something spreading. There is nothing more important in the universe when it comes to spreading than that we who are Jesus' followers should be spreading God's love, spreading the Gospel message, spreading God's provision He gives us to give unto others, spreading encouragement and support and kindness and goodness and generosity and mercy and grace, spreading help with understanding and living by the Bible, etc. And most assuredly we should be spreading THANKSGIVING for and to God!

When we express Thanksgiving to God in the presence of others, I believe we are sharing the love, hope, light, joy, and Truth of the Lord! And I believe we are spreading how humbling and exciting it is to PRAISE THE LORD! When I'm talking to people who love the Lord and tell me how thankful they are to Him, this to me is contagious. Thanksgiving to the Lord can and should be contagious, don't you think? Please help spread the love of Jesus and the Gospel message – and THANKSGIVING TO THE LORD! Thank you, Lord! Thank you, oh Lord! Let this very message be contagious!

"And he hath put a new song in my mouth, *even* praise unto our God: many shall see *it,* and fear, and shall trust in the LORD." Psalms 40:3 KJV

...

praise the Lord! ——————∞∞∞—————— hallelujah!

♥ My Jesus Journal Time! ♥

praise the Lord! ———ooo——— hallelujah!

#72

When People Don't Say Thank You

Have you ever gone really far out of your way, made a big sacrifice, and had great hope and expectation in giving someone a gift? Hoping and expecting the person would super appreciate your love, kindness, and generosity – and give you a big THANK YOU? I know. We're supposed to be so loving and giving that we don't care about getting a Thank You. But if you're honest with yourself, don't you sometimes want to get some appreciation, or at the very least acknowledgement, of what you gave? If I'm honest, in my humanness, and my still needing to grow in humility and generosity, sometimes I still care about being thanked. And when I don't get that Thank You, it can hurt some. In the past, it hurt lots. So here is my question.

If it hurts us humans to not be appreciated and thanked, and to not have our loving and giving acknowledged, how much do you suppose it must hurt the heart of God when He is the most loving person and the greatest Giver and the one who has made the greatest sacrifice in the universe? Think of all He has done, is doing, and will do for all of humanity INCLUDING YOURSELF, and imagine how He must feel when we take Him and His gifts and blessings for granted and don't take the love, time, and care to THANK THE LORD on an ongoing basis! This message is convicting for me. Is it for you? Oh, friend, let us grow! Let us grow big in our THANKSGIVING TO GOD!

"Praise ye the LORD. Praise the LORD, O my soul. While I live will I praise the LORD: I will sing praises unto my God while I have any being."
Psalms 146:1-2 KJV

...

praise the Lord! ———•○○○•——— hallelujah!

♥ My Jesus Journal Time! ♥

#73

Don't Forget to Say THANK YOU!

I pray all the time. I can't imagine living without praying. I love absolutely love to commune with God. I love to pray to Him, to seek Him, to cry out to Him, and yes, admittedly, I love to BEG HIM. When I'm desperate, the Lord knows. I have been known to really, really, really BEG God in prayer. But this message isn't about begging God. It's a warning NOT to do what sometimes I do after I pray to the Lord.

Take, for instance, this morning when I was bent down on the ground changing paralyzed ministry dog Miss Mercy's diaper. Yesterday I BEGGED God to heal the mild back problem I have had over days past. Caring for a paralyzed dog, including lifting her, can be a challenge with a back issue. So can walking which I LOVE to do because that's my favorite time to spend in God's presence praying, seeking Him, praising, worshiping, hearing Him, etc. So know what happened as I knelt down on the ground? I realized God had made my back a zillion times better, and I *remembered* to THANK HIM!

Here comes the warning. I can't tell you how many times I have BEGGED God for something but then when He answered my cries FORGOTTEN TO THANK HIM! We SHOULD NOT FORGET TO THANK GOD! We should *remember* to thank Him!

It's not that I don't believe God is worthy of my Thanksgiving 24-7 forever, mind you. It's just that sometimes I just plain old forget. And that's not very loving, is it? I believe in our love for and Thanksgiving to God we should make a big point of remembering to say THANK YOU LORD and to PRAISE HIM FOREVERMORE!

"Wherefore David blessed the LORD before all the congregation: and David said, Blessed *be* thou, LORD God of Israel our father, for ever and ever. Thine, O LORD, *is* the greatness, and the power, and the glory, and the victory, and the majesty: for all *that is* in the heaven and in the earth *is thine;* thine *is* the kingdom, O LORD, and thou art exalted as head above all. Both riches and honour *come* of thee, and thou reignest over all; and in thine hand *is* power and might; and in thine hand *it is* to make great, and to give strength unto all. Now therefore, our God, we thank thee, and praise thy glorious name. 1 Chron. 29:10-13 KJV

praise the Lord! ———∞∞——— hallelujah!

♥ My Jesus Journal Time! ♥

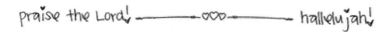

praise the Lord! ———ooo——— hallelujah!

#74

Don't Forget the Lord!

In the verses below, Moses whom God used to help deliver the Israelites out of bondage in Egypt WARNS THE PEOPLE. How so? He tells them when God blesses them beyond measure in the land He will give them NOT TO FORGET GOD. Moses doesn't tell them not to forget simply what God did for them. He tells them not to forget him period! Wow! Not only can we forget to thank God! We can also forget Him altogether! This is tragic, and this is wrong. And we need to be ultra careful NOT TO FORGET GOD – AND not to forget what Has done for us and to be thankful!

How could they possibly forget God? After all, God miraculously freed them from heinous bondage. After all, God is the one who promised the Israelites blessings beyond belief. Could they and would they forget? Better question. Never mind the Israelites. You can read in the Bible what happened to them after they came out of bondage. What about you and me? Would you agree sometimes God miraculously frees us, delivers us, heals us, rescues us, protects, etc. and blesses us in all sorts of ways and then not only do we forget to THANK HIM but sometimes we rush off to enjoy our blessings and forget Him altogether at least for little bits of time if not for long periods?

I believe this warning is as much for us as it was for them. Let us not ever, ever, ever forget the Lord, let us never forget His goodness, and let us never forget to say THANK YOU LORD!

"And it shall be, when the LORD thy God shall have brought thee into the land which he sware unto thy fathers, to Abraham, to Isaac, and to Jacob, to give thee great and goodly cities, which thou buildedst not, And houses full of all good *things,* which thou filledst not, and wells digged, which thou diggedst not, vineyards and olive trees, which thou plantedst not; when thou shalt have eaten and be full; *Then* beware lest thou forget the LORD, which brought thee forth out of the land of Egypt, from the house of bondage." Deuteronomy 6:10-12 KJV

...

praise the Lord! ———•◦◦◦•——— hallelujah!

My Jesus Journal Time!

Dear friend,

When I realized how long the next message I had written was and that it wouldn't fit into how I have set up this book to be with messages on even pages and Jesus Journal time on odd pages so they go together, I pondered what I could do. Quickly I realized I had a wonderful opportunity to add into this book a very special blessing. A photo of my beloved paralyzed ministry dogs Mr. Simeon (the big beautiful hound) and Miss Mercy. The Lord used them countless times over the years to bring me into the lives of people on the streets, on the beach, at hotels, in vets' offices, etc. to whom I was blessed to give my *Finding the Light Gospel* tract, talk to about the Lord Jesus Christ, pray for, minister to, etc. As of the writing of this book, I tragically lost my precious Mr. Simeon about a little over a year ago and my beautiful Miss Mercy – along with Gracie – is still with me. God is using Miss Mercy and Gracie in the same way, but there was nothing like going out with my 2 wheelchair ministry dogs. I hope you are blessed seeing the picture and inspired by the message that goes with it.

love & blessings, lara

On the Road for Jesus

lara love ♡

helping people find & follow Him

#75

But God I'm Grieving!

One of the greatest lessons I've learned about Thanksgiving, albeit one of the hardest, was when I tragically lost my long-time paralyzed ministry dog Mr. Simeon who was truly one of the absolute greatest blessings in my life. I lost him a bit over a year ago, and I was so bonded to that beautiful dog if it were not for Jesus I am positive I would not have made it through the loss. My heart is still crushed, but God carries me forward.

Mr. Simeon was found by a young woman after being run over by a car. She thought he was dead but he lifted his head off the ground. A year later, she still had him. She asked me to take him since I did dog rescue work. I said I couldn't. I had tons of dogs. I offered to meet him though and give advice. She had been thinking of euthanizing him. He was in horrible shape when I met him. He was being neglected in his rescuer's home. Emaciated, skin infection, ear infection if I recall, unbelievably long toenails, and laying alone on the floor surrounded with feces everywhere. The young woman agreed to let me take him to my vet's office and then return him. There was no turning back. With the young woman's permission, at the advice of the vet and at the leading of the Lord, I kept Mr. Simeon for years to come.

He died tragically one night in my hotel room. He was elderly and had had an amazing life but I never thought I would lose him that night nor truly ever. He was one of God's greatest gifts ever to me. He couldn't move more than a few inches without my help and relied on me for everything. He was also hugely spoiled, my fault of course, and "talked", yes talked, my ears off. When he wanted something, he told me. I remember being in the shower and hearing him "talk" because he wanted me to come back and be with him. Losing him broke me, not being able to take him on wheelchair walks with his long-time buddy paralyzed ministry dog Miss Mercy was heartbreaking. Still is, all this time later.

Know what happened almost immediately after the loss? The Lord compelled me to be THANKFUL. What? Thankful? In the midst of grief like that? Seriously? YES! God made me realize partly back then and then over time I should be thankful for all the years

He gave me with Mr. Simeon, for giving me a few extra years after he had almost died some years after getting him, for Mr. Simeon passing away with me there rather than my having to take him to a vet to euthanize him, for Mr. Simeon not going through a long painful disease like cancer like many of my other dogs over the years, for God's mercy on me for the times I fell short with Mr. Simeon and my other dogs when I in my sin lost my temper, for Mr. Simeon and the other dogs forgiving me when I fell short and didn't love them the way I desperately wanted to, and, most of all, for THE LORD HIMSELF and my relationship with Him and for all His endless blessings including for God's love and comfort for that incredible loss as well as for all the other losses I have gone through.

Less than 24 hours after losing Mr. Simeon, I was able to praise the Lord. Thanking God in the midst of our sorrow and grief does not mean we don't hurt. But it does mean we acknowledge the Lord and His amazingness through it all and thank Him for all that we should be thankful for – most of all FOR THE LORD!

I miss my Mr. Simeon like I just lost him yesterday. The sadness is deep inside me and hasn't gone away. But in God's strength I carry on loving and serving Him with all my heart, being thankful to God, and pressing on in fulfilling my life's calling to help people become and remain totally devoted followers of the Lord Jesus Christ.

Probably one of the last things in the world any of us would in our human nature consider when we're grieving a great loss is to be thankful to the Lord and to express our Thanksgiving to Him.

I believe losing Mr. Simeon marked a big turning point in my life. I believe the Lord used that incredible loss I experienced as an opportunity for me to learn to do something so vital in our seasons of loss. To be thankful to the Lord for all that we have to be thankful for – most especially for the Lord and including for the time the Lord gave us with those we have loved and lost.

"Let every thing that hath breath praise the LORD. Praise ye the LORD." Psalms 150:6 KJV

praise the Lord! ———ᴑᴑᴑ——— hallelujah!

My Jesus Journal Time!

praise the Lord! ——ooo—— hallelujah!

#76

Thank God for HEAVEN!

I used to pridefully judge people who talked and sang all the time about heaven as though they were fools to not simply figure out how to enjoy their lives now and should stop all this focus-on-heaven stuff. Now, for two humongous reasons, I can understand their extreme focus on heaven. First, many like myself have dealt with such challenging lives on this earth that it is a relief and great joy to realize that we who follow Jesus can look forward to being with God forever in a place with no pain, sorrow, sickness, incest, disease, disabilities, violence, rape, hatred, prejudice, war, hospitals, dying, etc. where all will be perfect and wonderful and easy and comfortable and filled with love and joy and peace and praise and worship and God's goodness. Second, whether our lives on this earth are incredibly easy or terribly hard or somewhere in between, we who are God's followers get to look forward to spending forever and ever in His face-to-face glorious and splendorous magnificent presence! With all of His children in perfect unity!

Let us thank the Lord! Let us praise the Lord! Let us worship the Lord! Let us offer to Him our Thanksgiving for the promise of heaven with Him forevermore for all who repent, believe in Jesus Christ as Lord and in His death and resurrection, and commit our lives wholly and forever to Him, AMEN!

"And I heard a great voice out of heaven saying, Behold, the tabernacle of God *is* with men, and he will dwell with them, and they shall be his people, and God himself shall be with them, *and be* their God. And God shall wipe away all tears from their eyes; and there shall be no more death, neither sorrow, nor crying, neither shall there be any more pain: for the former things are passed away. And he that sat upon the throne said, Behold, I make all things new. And he said unto me, Write: for these words are true and faithful. And he said unto me, It is done. I am Alpha and Omega, the beginning and the end. I will give unto him that is athirst of the fountain of the water of life freely. He that overcometh shall inherit all things; and I will be his God, and he shall be my son." Revelation 21:3-7 KJV

praise the Lord! ——— ∞∞ ——— hallelujah!

♥ My Jesus Journal Time! ♥

praise the Lord! ———ooo——— hallelujah!

#77

God's People Provision

When I think of God's provision, and being thankful to Him for it, I have usually thought of His provision of things like food, clothing, shelter, clean drinking water, money to pay bills, a car to get where I'm supposed to go, etc. But what I have sorely lacked is Thanksgiving to God for HIS PROVISION OF PEOPLE.

Believe it or not, God brought this message to mind when I was thinking of police officers. See, I have been on the road full-time as of the writing of this book for about 4.5 years with my special needs ministry dogs. Most of the time staying in budget hotels where I have done lots of my ministry work along with small apartments for a short while twice in New York City where hotels are too high priced and not conducive to special needs dogs. Given the state of this world, and how many live in rebellion against God, in most of the places I have stayed there has been drug selling, drug using, people who are homeless, alcoholics, suicidal people, domestic abuse, violence, prostitution, fighting, etc. Perfect opportunities for ministry work, but pretty scary, uncomfortable, overwhelming.

I realized I had taken for granted God's provision of police officers to help me feel and be safe. Later I realized, wow. I have fallen terribly far short over the years in thanking God for ALL His provision of people who have loved me, blessed me, encouraged me, prayed for me, helped me, supported me, walked alongside me, helped me to grow, been patient with me, been my family and friends, been generous with me, etc. My favorite person in the universe, of course, is the Lord. My first love. My God, King, Savior, master, counselor, comforter, helper, healer, advocate, and very best friend. Oh, how exceedingly, exceedingly thankful to the Lord I am for all His love and provision – people included! Even the difficult, hurtful, challenging ones whom He has used to teach me, test me, grow me, refine me, purify me, etc. Oh, thank you Lord! Let us thank God for people, friend! Let us glorify God with our praise!

"Whoso offereth praise glorifieth me: and to him that ordereth *his* conversation *aright* will I shew the salvation of God." Psalms 50:23 KJV

praise the Lord! ———•ᴑᴑᴑ——— hallelujah!

♥ My Jesus Journal Time! ♥

#78

My Prayer of Praise

I LOVE, LOVE, LOVE to write, so it is no wonder I LOVE to write prayers to God, praise to God, questions to God, pour out my heart to God, etc. Today is Thanksgiving Day morning, and one would think I would be totally lonely and depressed. I have no Thanksgiving Day plans. One friend invited me over but knows I prefer to be on my own on holidays. So she offered to drop off some Thanksgiving Day food. The only people I will likely see are the staff and guests at my current hotel on the road for Jesus. And I will be with my sweet special needs ministry doggies Miss Mercy and Grace of course.

Am I lonely? Not in the least! I am thankful, and I am so excited that just about three days into writing this book I am already by God's grace more than half way through. Here is a bit of what I wrote the Lord this morning:

"Oh God, you are so good! So wonderful! So praiseworthy! I love you forever and ever, dear Father! Amen! I am excited beginning this new day with you, dear Lord! Help me to love and glorify you with every ounce of my heart now and forever, dear Lord. AMEN!" I also wrote this: "THANKSGIVING. Yes, Lord, and I am so thankful for YOU above all else. Thank you for this day and all the hope in it. You are my hope dear God."

Know what strikes me about these words that poured forth from my heart to thank the Lord? That I am ultra clear my greatest reason for Thanksgiving is God Himself. Is THE LORD your greatest reason for being thankful? I so hope so! And if He's not, please change your priorities. The Lord is to be our first love. And if He is not, we need to repent and raise Him up to where He belongs in our hearts and lives. NUMBER ONE! Number one for whom and to whom we should be thankful? The LORD!

"Unto the angel of the church of Ephesus write;...Nevertheless I have *somewhat* against thee, because thou hast left thy first love. Remember therefore from whence thou art fallen, and repent, and do the first works; or else I will come unto thee quickly, and will remove thy candlestick out of his place, except thou repent." Revelation 2:1-5 KJV

...

praise the Lord! ———∞∞∞——— hallelujah!

❤ My Jesus Journal Time! ❤

praise the Lord! ⎯⎯⎯ ∞ ⎯⎯⎯ hallelujah!

#79

Your Number One Hope

If you've already read that I wrote the Lord on Thanksgiving Day these words, "Thank you for this day and all the hope in it. You are my hope dear God," or if you know me well, or even if you've known me for just a few minutes, it usually doesn't take knowing me or hearing me or reading my writing for very long to know that the Lord is my first love. My highest priority. My greatest desire. And He doesn't just give me hope. I don't just hope in His promises as He reveals to us in the Bible. I don't just look forward to the hope of heaven. THE LORD JESUS CHRIST IS MY HOPE.

Everything and everyone on this planet could be gone. Heaven could no longer exist. I would be devastated beyond imagination. But nobody and nothing can take away my hope. Because my hope is THE LORD Himself. And He, friend, is FOREVER. And He, friend, is LOVE (1 John 4:8). And He, friend, is more beautiful and wonderful and magnificent and phenomenal and awesome and amazing and satisfying and kinder and more compassionate and more tender and more true and faithful and loyal and giving and generous and splendorous and glorious than anything or anyone in the universe!

The Lord Jesus Christ is my everlasting HOPE. Is He yours?

I was hopeless for decades. Then I had hope. Some hope. But it wasn't until I truly turned to the Lord as my number one HOPE that I came to have the Thanksgiving in my heart I have today for the HOPE in my life. For my Thanksgiving isn't for just any hope. I am forever thankful to my eternal HOPE. JESUS!

How about you? Is He your hope forever?

"Now the God of hope fill you with all joy and peace in believing, that ye may abound in hope, through the power of the Holy Ghost." Romans 15:13 KJV

"But sanctify the Lord God in your hearts: and *be* ready always to *give* an answer to every man that asketh you a reason of the hope that is in you with meekness and fear:" 1 Peter 3:15 KJV

praise the Lord! ⸺ooo⸺ hallelujah!

My Jesus Journal Time!

#80

I Didn't Even Notice!

I've been writing so incredibly much over the past few days that I am extra thankful for the little break I just took on this chilly southern late fall morning to walk my special needs ministry dog Gracie and to gulp in some fresh air. To my great surprise the sun is shining brightly which I simply didn't expect. I felt a little glee in my heart about the sun, felt a little disappointed I won't be out in it much today because I am compelled to press on in writing this book today, then realized something important I feel I need to share with you and hurried back inside – to WRITE!

I am 54 years old. Fifty-four times 365 is a whole lot of days, weeks, months, and years I have lived so far. Honestly, for most of those days – and years – as much as I LOVE sunshine and especially WARM sunshine and most especially WARM SUNSHINE on or near the beach, I have taken the sun for granted for most of my life! I assumed it would always be there, and that when it didn't appear because of clouds and rain and such I assumed it would return eventually. But almost never in all these years have I thought to think, feel, and say, THANK YOU LORD FOR THE SUNSHINE! Hallelujah, PRAISE YOU GOD for the sun! And for every other blessing you, God, have ever given me and every other human being on this earth. Oh, thank you God!

What do you suppose would happen if all of us on earth stopped taking God's blessings for granted, overlooking His goodness, and forgetting and neglecting to praise Him? And started making a really big really conscious effort to live a lifestyle of total devotion to God – including THANKSGIVING – for the rest of our lives and forevermore? Can you imagine how much this would delight the Lord? I so want to be much more humble, be much more joyful, be much more loving, be much more praising and thanking God for every single breath & blessing God gives me. You, too, friend?

"Praise ye him, sun and moon: praise him, all ye stars of light." Psalms 148:3

"From the rising of the sun unto the going down of the same the LORD'S name *is* to be praised." Psalms 113:3

praise the Lord! ——○○○—— hallelujah!

♥ My Jesus Journal Time! ♥

#81

Bringing God PLEASURE

I have been such a self-centered person for so much of my life. I was so consumed with pleasure-seeking for a good number of those years that I could hardly have conceived of bringing pleasure to someone else. Unless there was something I would get in return whether it be praise, attention, validation, big thankyou's, a relationship I wanted, someone's care and kindness, etc. I have since been learning about what it really means to deny self and love others, and most of all I have been learning about how to really love God. So sadly, I carried over my self-centeredness into my relationship with God.

I tragically came under false so-called prosperity gospel teaching whereby I was taught following God is all about waving our magic wands, having enough faith, and getting everything we want from God. I was essentially trained to believe God is here to love and serve us not we are here to love and serve and glorify God and of course to be loved by God also. I was under it's-all-about-me teaching, and praise God He delivered me out of it. Now I understand if we really love God with all our hearts as we are commanded to do, we will long to love Him and we will yearn to please and honor and glorify Him. We will hunger to bring Him pleasure and go to great lengths no matter the cost to our flesh to bring Him joy, love, pleasure, praise, and glory!

What does this have to do with Thanksgiving? I would think that God takes great pleasure when His children go to great lengths to PRAISE HIM, to THANK HIM, to WORSHIP HIM, to SPEND TIME WITH HIM. When we make it a priority to live with Thanksgiving to God ever in our hearts, mouths, and actions. Let us bring the Lord delight, my friend, let us bring Him delight and pleasure and praise and joy and honor and obedience and humble fellowship and glory! Praise the Lord!

"For it is God which worketh in you both to will and to do of *his* good pleasure." Philippians 2:13 KJ

"Thou art worthy, O Lord, to receive glory and honour and power: for thou hast created all things, and for thy pleasure they are and were created." Revelation 4:11 KJV

praise the Lord! ———ooo——— hallelujah!

My Jesus Journal Time!

#82

A Challenge to the Churches

Some people do great with this. I don't. At all. You know. The sit-stand-sit-stand-sing-sit-stand-pray-make-sure-you-don't-sing-for-more-than-10-minutes-everything-at-Sunday-church-service-has-to-be-pre-planned-and-run-like-clockwork-or-else. I am not here to judge. I believe God sees our hearts. If we're genuinely loving, praising, worshiping Him, etc. "in spirit and in truth", very strict programmed church scheduling or not, I believe God is blessed with sincere love and adoration for and of Him.

But I wonder is it possible God is offended and dishonored and disheartened and perhaps even disgusted by what is going on in so many modern day American churches with the extreme programming, bright lights, smoky stages, video screens, comedy, expensive stage sets, entertainment, in-church gyms, well-rehearsed worship music with the choir facing the congregation rather than everyone looking upward worshiping God, with Christmas decorations when Christmas trees go against God's Word, etc.?

What if all this were stripped away? What would remain? What would He see in our hearts? And hear coming from our mouths? I wonder what it would look like if all the churches all across the land, and world, would lay aside our man-made plans and let the Holy Spirit lead the way. Some churches do this, mind you. And I would imagine the first Christians likely did.

What if we prayed as long as we're led to pray? What if we sang the songs God puts on our hearts unrehearsed not with the congregation facing the choir and vice versa but with all of us looking heavenward and singing with great passion to God? What if we let people give their testimonies when they yearned to tell the congregation what God had done even if the yearning came at the time the third song is normally programmed to be sung? What if instead of bowing our heads and shutting our eyes when the pastor asks if anyone wants to commit his or her life to the Lord we all had our eyes wide open and people started crying out to God with godly sorrow for their sins desperately calling on the Lord to have mercy on them like they did in the times of great revival long ago?

What if the pastors preached the whole Truth of the Bible leaving nothing out even if all the people ran away when the pastor preached on sin, heaven, and hell and called the people to repentance and a life of obedience and holiness. What if the pastors didn't sugar coat God's Truth to please the people and keep the church pews filled?

And what if when it comes to Thanksgiving, whether we're in the church building or out walking our dogs or sitting on our front porches or crying in our jail cells or smooshed up in a tiny bunk bed at our homeless shelters or driving cross country to a funeral service thinking about God we simply and sincerely started calling out to God in our hearts or even boisterously aloud to tell Him how THANKFUL we are?

What if our Thanksgiving alone with God and in the presence of others poured from our hearts, mouths, and lives continually as well it should?

What if we got rid of all our human-made regulations and rules and restrictions and as long as we did things "decently and in order (1 Cor. 14:14)" to honor God we lay all the human traditions and programs and agendas and church comforts aside and simply humbled ourselves before God almighty and loved and praised and thanked and worshiped the Lord with every single ounce of our hearts?

And what if we all went all out getting out of the pews and going beyond the church walls to tell the world about the Lord Jesus Christ and how to have forever life with God instead of spend eternity apart from Him in torment in hell and the lake of fire?

May all who read this message and I humble ourselves, cry out to God, and make any and all changes in our hearts and lives so God is loved, honored, praised, obeyed, served, thanked, and glorified by us this very day and forevermore! Glory be to the Lord! Amen!

"But the hour cometh, and now is, when the true worshippers shall worship the Father in spirit and in truth: for the Father seeketh such to worship him. God *is* a Spirit: and they that worship him must worship *him* in spirit and in truth." John 4:23-24 KJV

...

Please find another little letter

from my heart to yours on the next page!

praise the Lord! ——ooo—— hallelujah!

Another Little Letter from Lara

Dear friend,

This message you just read is extra near & dear to my heart! I have grieved greatly over so much of what I have seen & heard about in modern day American church culture. I am afraid many have gotten way off course. So many it seems are more concerned with comfort & pleasing self than with forsaking all to follow Jesus & love, praise, honor, serve, obey, thank, & glorify God no matter the cost to our flesh.

So many professing to believe in Jesus Christ as Lord are lukewarm. So many seem spiritually dead. My heart's cry is that all who call Jesus Lord will humble ourselves and forsake all for Jesus. And my heart's cry is that all who do not yet call Him Lord will repent, believe in Him as Lord and in His death and resurrection, & commit their lives to God wholly and forever. That all will live totally devoted to the Lord Jesus Christ forevermore. And that in so doing our hearts and lives will overflow with endless Thanksgiving to God almighty!

Would you consider using your Jesus Journal Time space this time around to pray to God and seek Him and listen for His voice speaking to your heart concerning where you stand with Him? Are you totally sold out to Him? Are you entirely surrendered? Do you live and breathe to love and glorify Him? Is Thanksgiving to God a wonderfully and blessed continual priority and part of your life? Oh, may this be so!

love & blessings,

lara

"And unto the angel of the church of the Laodiceans write; These things saith the Amen, the faithful and true witness, the beginning of the creation of God; I know thy works, that thou art neither cold nor hot: I would thou wert cold or hot. So then because thou art lukewarm, and neither cold nor hot, I will spue thee out of my mouth." Rev. 3:14-16 KJV

praise the Lord! ———•∞•——— hallelujah!

♥ My Jesus Journal Time! ♥

praise the Lord! ———ooo——— hallelujah!

#83
The Cost of Serving Christ

The cost of loving and serving the Lord with all my heart which for me has included selling my little house not far from the beach, giving most everything away, and going on the road full-time as a single middle-aged woman with my special needs ministry dogs in a world filled with wickedness beyond measure, danger, a pandemic, and a zillion challenges of one sort or another, has been NOTHING compared with the cost so many of Christ's followers have faced in loving and serving the Lord with all their hearts. People get their heads chopped off and are tortured for sharing the Gospel.

What I have faced on the streets and at the hotels of America in the way of filth, vomit, men going to the bathroom on the streets, danger, criminals, half naked people, being yelled and cursed at, sticking my finger on someone's needle in New York City, being alone with a violent criminal at a hotel unable to get to my dogs, helping people overdosing, being hated for loving and following Jesus, giving up a social life for Jesus, not having a traditional salary so I can be wholly available for God, being far away from loved ones, living in much solitude to spend time with the Lord and write when I'm not out telling the world about Jesus, this is NOTHING compared with the cost others pay. But it has still been a cost to my flesh.

Truth is I wouldn't return to a life of comfort and ease for anything. I would choose the Lord Jesus Christ and my calling for Him over comfort without hesitation. I would give up all I have been asked to give up all over again just to know I am bringing even a single ounce of love, joy, honor, praise and glory to God and that I am helping even a single soul to know and follow the Lord forever. Oh, I am so, so, so very thankful.

May you forsake ALL for the Lord – and be THANKFUL!

"But what things were gain to me, those I counted loss for Christ. Yea doubtless, and I count all things *but* loss for the excellency of the knowledge of Christ Jesus my Lord: for whom I have suffered the loss of all things, and do count them *but* dung, that I may win Christ," Phil. 3:7-8 KJV praise the Lord! ——∞∞—— hallelujah!

♥ My Jesus Journal Time! ♥

#84

Thanking God for HEALTH!

I fall short in every area of my life including when it comes to being thankful for my health and God's provision for my health. I believe I am not alone in this. When we're sick, we can be quick to moan and groan. When we're waiting for test results or get a tough diagnosis, we can be quick to pray for healing. But is it possible we need to improve in our Thanksgiving to God concerning our health and well-being?

Do we thank the Lord for the health we do have? Or, if we're nearing the end of our lives, do we thank Him for the good health He gave us in the past? Or for the little bit of health with which He is still blessing us? Oh, sure, we may have health issues. Some may even have really hard ones. But is it possible we're falling short in being thankful to God for what is working right in our bodies and minds? And for those of us who have lots of aspects of our health not working, are we thanking Him for the people He sends to love us, help us, pray for us, care for us, show compassion toward us, etc.?

And what about the healthcare industry? I tend to complain about how much the healthcare system has declined. Seems it's become one big business and it's harder to find doctors who will take the time to really spend with their patients. To find genuine compassion coupled with medical expertise. To deal with the insurance companies, this can be hard. And, oh, the medical billing companies, the hospital systems that have taken over whole regions, I am quick to complain about this and how frustrated and stressed I am when a medical bill is all messed up and nobody will help me properly – for months!

But how quick – or slow - are we to be thankful that we can get medical care, that medication does exist, that there are some really good doctors, that we have good hospitals in America, for the times God heals us, for the health help He provides for us, etc.? Oh, let us be thankful. Let us declare to the Lord and show the Lord our Thanksgiving!

"O sing unto the LORD a new song: sing unto the LORD, all the earth. Sing unto the LORD, bless his name; shew forth his salvation from day to day. Declare his glory among the heathen, his wonders among all people." Psalms 96:1-3 KJV

praise the Lord! ———•○○○•——— hallelujah!

♥ My Jesus Journal Time! ♥

#85

Blessed to Be Forgiven

We're all sinners. None of us deserve God's love. None of us deserve His forgiveness. None of us deserve His salvation. None of us deserve everlasting life with Him. The punishment we deserve for our sins and would get if it were not for Jesus is death, hell, and the lake of fire and forever in torment apart from God. The Bible says we're blessed to be forgiven by God.

My question is, are we thankful? And how thankful are we? Or is it possible we take for granted God's forgiveness and our salvation through Jesus? Do we undermine what exactly God has done for us? I would imagine we may, but we don't need to continue to do so.

I am here to remind you, and to remind me, let's never take Jesus' death and resurrection for granted. Let us always be thankful for the Lord's sacrifice, for His astounding love, for His forgiveness, and for His promise of forever life with Him.

For those who turn from our sins, believe in Jesus Christ as Lord and in His death and resurrection and truly turn our lives over to God and His ways, we receive God's forgiveness and the promise of everlasting life with Him! And His very Holy Spirit comes to live inside us!

Do we really realize how unfathomably blessed we are? Oh, we should be rejoicing! And thankful forevermore! Amen!

"Blessed *is he whose* transgression *is* forgiven, *whose* sin *is* covered." Psalms 32:1 KJV

...

praise the Lord! ———ooo——— hallelujah!

♥ My Jesus Journal Time! ♥

#86

A Thankful Heart

If God could see inside your heart right now, what would He see? Would He see Thanksgiving? God can see inside our hearts! He sees everything we have inside them! Let's make sure what He sees is pure and pleasing to Him. Anything that's not, let's get rid of it.

If the person you love most in life were coming for a visit, wouldn't you work hard to make your place clean and welcoming? Okay, some of us like myself aren't so big on fixing up our physical places for people to visit. But you get the point. We should love nobody and nothing more than we love the Lord, and we should strive to keep our "places" clean for Jesus at all times. Ever humbling ourselves and purifying ourselves.

The Spirit of God lives inside His followers. He sees EVERYTHING we have inside us. Let's not just get rid of what needs to be gone. Let's be filled with what pleases the Lord. And let this always, always, always include a THANKFUL-TO-GOD HEART! And a THANKFUL-TO-GOD ATTITUDE! May our hearts ALWAYS be filled with Thanksgiving to God! And, when they are not, let us repent quickly and fill up our hearts with THANKSGIVING TO THE LORD!

"Know ye not that ye are the temple of God, and *that* the Spirit of God dwelleth in you?" 1 Corinthians 3:16 KJV

...

praise the Lord! ———ᴏᴏᴏ——— hallelujah!

My Jesus Journal Time!

#87

The Joy of Thanksgiving

Is there anything in your life you are extra thankful for? I don't think I've ever thought about Thanksgiving as much as I have since I started writing this book! For whom and what I am most thankful? The Lord and my forever relationship with Him and the Bible! Whom and what else? People I love! Well, God has given me a love for all people. I am thankful truly for all people. And I am extra thankful for those closest to me like my Mom and Dad and brother and aunt! And my beautiful friends! And I am so incredibly thankful for my precious ministry dogs! My ministry work for God! My writing! All God's provision! Hope! Joy! Kindness! Peace! Compassion! People who care! The warm sunshine! The beach!

I am smiling as I write this. I believe our Thanksgiving to God brings Him joy, and I believe being thankful brings us joy also! Feeling joyful as you read this? Why not spend some time thinking about – and maybe writing about - what makes you thankful! Please be sure to tell the Lord! As much as Thanksgiving can make us joyful, let's make sure bringing God joy & Thanksgiving is our highest priority when it comes to thankfulness!

"But let the righteous be glad; let them rejoice before God: yea, let them exceedingly rejoice." Psalms 68:3 KJV

...

praise the Lord! ——————∞∞———— hallelujah!

♥ My Jesus Journal Time! ♥

#88

She's So Negative!

I know someone I truly love beyond measure but whom sometimes I want to keep a little distance from because the person can be pretty negative. Our conversations usually start off positive, but then they can drift pretty quickly into the person saying one negative thing or another. Truthfully, for me it's like looking in the mirror. The person doesn't believe in the Lord, but I'm sad to say I spent plenty of years believing in the Lord and being totally negative. I can still become negative in a heartbeat if I'm not careful, and I have to be really vigilant in not falling into negativity and repent quickly when I do.

Even though it's not fun to listen to people's negativity, I'm actually thankful I have had this experience of listening to it. I now realize how much I have hurt others with my negativity most especially God and also countless others. I don't want to be thought of by others as a woman of negativity. I want to be seen and heard and thought of as a woman of Thanksgiving to God!

What I would really like is for people to think of me as a huge, huge lover of the Lord who is humble, loving, joyful, peaceful, kind, caring, compassionate, giving, generous, etc. – and THANKFUL TO THE LORD! I want to influence people with my attitude, what I say, what I write, and my actions in such a way they are encouraged to be totally devoted followers of the Lord Jesus Christ! And I want them to be inspired by me and my life and ministry to love, praise, honor, rejoice in, adore, sing to, worship, serve, obey, glorify, and THANK THE LORD forevermore!

My heart's cry for the person I shared about who can be negative is that the person repents and becomes a forever follower of Jesus who will thank and praise the Lord forevermore. This, friend, is my heart's cry for us all!

"And every creature which is in heaven, and on the earth, and under the earth, and such as are in the sea, and all that are in them, heard I saying, Blessing, and honour, and glory, and power, *be* unto him that sitteth upon the throne, and unto the Lamb for ever and ever." Revelation 5:13 KJV

praise the Lord! ———ooo——— hallelujah!

My Jesus Journal Time!

#89

Thankful for Growing Pains

I was a late bloomer as a girl. I grew and developed much later than my classmates. I thought I would always be short and undeveloped. God took care of that. I eventually grew and developed. And I had growing pains along the way. I remember having leg cramps at night as a girl. I suppose that was part of the growing I had so wanted to do. Same thing happened as a believer in Jesus. I wanted to grow in my relationship with the Lord, but I started off really slow. Eventually I started growing. And there have been lots of growing pains along the way. Lots of learning, lots of being tested, lots of trials, lots of needing to be humbled, lots of need for repentance, lots of crying out to God to help and change and grow me. He has, and He is, and I know He will continue to do so.

The growing pains so to speak have been really hard. So much of the time I didn't think I would make it through all the refining and such. But God has helped me through it all. And now, at long last, I can look back and say I am so very thankful to God for not giving up on me, for all He has done to bring me to where I am now, for how He has brought me closer and closer to Himself, and for how He uses me so much in others' lives to help them become and remain totally devoted to Him. And, believe it or not, I am thankful for the growing pains. I am thankful for what God has chosen to do along the way to lead me to where I am.

It's not so easy to be thankful for growing pains. But I believe when we look at the big picture of learning how to follow Jesus, we can choose Thanksgiving for all that is the will of God. Growing pains included.

"But grow in grace, and *in* the knowledge of our Lord and Saviour Jesus Christ. To him *be* glory both now and for ever. Amen." 2 Peter 3:18 KJV

...

praise the Lord! ———ooo——— hallelujah!

♥ My Jesus Journal Time! ♥

#90

The Silly Starfish Story

Many people who have known me over the years don't know I went to an Ivy League university and planned to become a doctor. Not only was I totally turned off by chemistry, and not only would I likely never had made it through pre-med classes let alone made it into med school. But something that totally turned me off from wanting to be on the pre-med path I was on at the time was when a professor made the students learn the parts of a starfish. What did starfish have to do with becoming a doctor? That starfish assignment was the end of it all for me. The end of wanting to become a doctor anyway!

When I look back at my life, there were countless times I was totally off course. I was on the wrong pathway so much of the time. Before I believed in the Lord, and even once I came to believe in Him but wasn't yet totally devoted to Him, I was so often headed in the wrong direction. I am so thankful to God today that He had a plan all along for me and that He guided me over time onto the right pathway. His pathway for me.

There are no starfishes on my pathway now. No pre-med. No med school. No being a doctor. No lots of other things I thought would be part of my future. The Lord lovingly and mercifully redirected me to where I am today. Totally His. Doing what He created me to do. Loving and serving Him with all my heart in my life and ministry.

Let us be thankful for all the love and care and patience God has with us as He directs us to and down the pathway He has created us to walk down. And let us be thankful for any and all redirecting He does throughout the course of our lives. Let us be thankful for His leading. Let us be thankful for His will for us. Let us be thankful for His purpose for us. Let us be thankful for His love for us. Let us be thankful for the path He sets us upon.

"The LORD *is* my shepherd; I shall not want. He maketh me to lie down in green pastures: he leadeth me beside the still waters. He restoreth my soul: he leadeth me in the paths of righteousness for his name's sake." Psalms 23:1-3 KJV

"Trust in the LORD with all thine heart; and lean not unto thine own understanding. In all thy ways acknowledge him, and he shall direct thy paths." Proverbs 3:5-6 KJV

praise the Lord! ———ꝏ——— hallelujah!

♥ My Jesus Journal Time! ♥

#91

Praising God in the Pain

I was taking my usual daily walk today with the Lord singing aloud to Him what was on my heart when I saw two parents with their kids happily bike riding. It is Thanksgiving Day, and I am on my own for the day writing. I could have cried when I saw that family. Family the way family should be and mine used to be. Decades ago, I was kicked out of my family for talking about something that happened long ago. Though God has blessedly restored some of my family, I am not allowed to see my Dad nor go inside my parents' house if he is home nor spend holidays with my family.

I will never be able to describe in words the emotional pain over the years. Only the Lord knows the depths of it because only He knows my exceeding love for my Dad and my desperate desire for decades to have had a close relationship with my dear Dad. So imagine my heart when I saw that family this Thanksgiving enjoying each other's company while I have spent the day alone with God and my beloved special needs ministry dogs writing and writing.

Know what I did that I would not have done until not so very long ago? I kept singing and praising God because I am so very thankful for so very much! I have so much reason to rejoice and be thankful to God! I am thankful for… Him, all my blessings, my family when it was intact, the love and mercy God has given me for my family, the part of my family He restored, my heart to pray for my Dad and other family members, having shared the Gospel with my family, God hearing my cries to Him for my family's salvation, health, safety, etc., my Dad knowing my love for him through my Mom, the opportunity to give him gifts and cards over the years, the few times he responded, God's love and comfort, how God has used what I have gone through to draw me to Himself, grow me, and to make me best able to love and help others – and for a zillion other reasons.

Each day, whether it's a good one or a really hard one, or somewhere in between, and yes, even in the pain, I do my best to choose joy and Thanksgiving. Will you?

"Rejoice in the Lord alway: *and* again I say, Rejoice." Phil. 4:4 KJV

praise the Lord! ———∞∞——— hallelujah!

♥ My Jesus Journal Time! ♥

#92

Another Opportunity

Maybe you've never written a whole book about Thanksgiving. I am guessing you probably haven't. I hadn't until now, and here I am getting closer and closer to finishing writing my first draft of the messages portion of this devotional-journal book. Oh, sure, I wrote a book called 365 Blessings jam packed with verses God led me to write about. But this book is all about being thankful. And one might think after just about 4 days of writing what is now 91 messages, all glory to the Lord, that I would run out of messages to write about Thanksgiving. Oh, not so. I so love how the Holy Spirit leads me in life and ministry including most assuredly in my writing. He gives me endless messages! Like this one about getting another opportunity. Something for which I am so thankful.

See, some people seem to get through life effortlessly. Without lots of mistakes. Without lots of problems. Without lots of missed opportunities. I, on the other hand, have had problems galore for as long as I can remember. I have done so much wrong, made so many mistakes, sinned so much, missed so many opportunities, so often been on the wrong path, well, you get the point. So I'm extra, extra thankful to the Lord that even when I have been on the wrong path and missed opportunities as a result, when I have repented, He has lovingly, mercifully, graciously, tenderly, taken me by the hand and led me forward in the right direction. His direction. And, in so doing, He has given me opportunities I didn't deserve to have and this time to get it right. Can you relate? If yes, please, please, please be thankful to the Lord for His tender love and mercy in all this!

Please note in these verses what Jesus says at the end to the people to whom He has given miracles. He hasn't given up on them! He gives them another opportunity in life, doesn't He? I encourage you to look up their full stories in the Bible!

"Afterward Jesus findeth him in the temple, and said unto him, Behold, thou art made whole: sin no more, lest a worse thing come unto thee." John 5:14

"She said, No man, Lord. And Jesus said unto her, Neither do I condemn thee: go, and sin no more." John 8:11

praise the Lord! ———∞∞∞——— hallelujah!

❤ My Jesus Journal Time! ❤

praise the Lord! ——ooo—— hallelujah!

#93

Jesus Took My Wheel

I was in the pickup truck passenger seat years ago when my then husband who was driving was in a rage. I was petrified to begin with and though I was then well accustomed to his rages never in a million years would have imagined a massive truck would be headed straight for us in what would have been a head-on collision. I am totally serious when I tell you I saw the wheel turn our vehicle out of the way though I am absolutely positive my then husband did not turn the wheel himself. I know without a shadow of doubt that the Lord took that wheel and saved our lives.

When I have periodically over the years recalled that miracle, I have been so thankful to God for His protection. But what I failed to see until this very day believe it or not is I have another reason to be so exceedingly thankful for what the Lord did that day. He saved me *so I could fulfill the purpose He has for me on this earth*. To fulfill my life's calling to help people to become and remain totally devoted followers of the Lord Jesus Christ. I was a broken pretty much hopeless mess in a devastatingly tough marriage all those years ago, but now all these years later by God's love, grace, power, and mercy, I am behind my own vehicle on the road full-time for Jesus and ministry. I am so thankful that He protected us that day, AND I am so thankful He is enabling me day by day now to fulfill my ministry for Him! The purpose for which He saved me!

In writing this, I am led by the Holy Spirit to consider something I don't believe I have ever thought about before. If we keep our hearts, ears, and eyes wide open to the Lord, I believe we can go to deeper and deeper levels of Thanksgiving and find more and more reasons to be thankful to the Lord and to express our Thanksgiving to Him with all our hearts!

"Who hath saved us, and called *us* with an holy calling, not according to our works, but according to his own purpose and grace, which was given us in Christ Jesus before the world began," 2 Timothy 1:9 KJV

...

praise the Lord! ⸻·ᴏᴐᴐ·⸻ hallelujah!

♥ My Jesus Journal Time! ♥

#94

From High Heels to Death Row

If you've met me in recent years and know my super simple lifestyle of being on the road for Jesus wearing mostly thrift shop clothes, living really economically, staying in low budget hotels and motels lots of people wouldn't want to go near, having few possessions, having no permanent residence as I go from place to place telling the world about Jesus, getting no regular salary, having no social life so I can be totally available to the Lord and ministry, etc. you may have a hard time believing this.

I am an Ivy League graduate who once worked in the Wall Street area copy editing financial publications, drinking to no end, "falling in love" with a still-married-but-supposedly-getting-divorced alcoholic after chasing after numerous other men in bars, and wearing high heels, stockings, and relatively expensive clothes. The short version of DECADES of my life is I was broken beyond human hope and repair.

Today I'm a totally devoted follower of Jesus. I live and breathe to love, serve, & glorify the Lord and help others do the same! The same sin-ridden broken woman who click-clicked in those heels in my years of ever-spiraling-downward brokenness who contemplated suicide on/off for about 20 years has been blessed to minister on death row a few times amid what is now years of incredible ministry opportunities. Talk about miraculous transformation!

I will be forever thankful for what God has done with me, is doing with me, has yet to do with me, and does through me to love and help others. I am here to encourage you who are reading this to be totally devoted to the Lord and to yield yourself completely to the transformative work He desires to do in your life! Be thankful and praise the Lord for what He will do when you yield yourself entirely to Him!

"I beseech you therefore, brethren, by the mercies of God, that ye present your bodies a living sacrifice, holy, acceptable unto God, *which is* your reasonable service. And be not conformed to this world: but be ye transformed by the renewing of your mind, that ye may prove what *is* that good, and acceptable, and perfect, will of God." Rom. 12:1-2 KJV

praise the Lord! ——————∞∞—————— hallelujah!

❤ My Jesus Journal Time! ❤

#95

Your Life's Story

If God gave each of us a piece of paper early in life and told us to write down everything we wanted our life story to be, to write down every dream, desire, wish, and want, to squeeze it all onto one page as best we were able, to map out our lives exactly the way we wanted and expected them to turn out, I wonder how many of us would write down exactly what God desires and has planned for our lives. What if we could put down our highest hopes for how our life's story will unfold, turn the paper in to God, and watch everything come to pass according to our will? I can't imagine. Can you?

My life has turned out so exceedingly different than I had ever hoped for and desired. But I wouldn't change my life story for anything in the world. I am living the life at long last God planned for me all along. And though it's so incredibly hard on my flesh to not have gotten most of what I wanted and to have lost so much of what I did want and did get, I wouldn't give up the plan God has had for my life all along for anything.

I am thankful beyond measure because God's plan is absolutely always the very best! My life story now that I have finally stopped living for me and at long last am living for God is the one He has chosen for me. I am humbled, blessed, and privileged – and so unbelievably thankful – that God is bringing to pass His will for my life. I am finally surrendered to Him as I should have been all along. I am so thankful for His will for me!

Are you fully surrendered to God and His will for your life? Are you living out the life story God created you to have? If not, will you surrender all to the Lord now? And will you choose to be THANKFUL for the plan and purpose God has for your life?

"For this cause we also, since the day we heard *it,* do not cease to pray for you, and to desire that ye might be filled with the knowledge of his will in all wisdom and spiritual understanding; That ye might walk worthy of the Lord unto all pleasing, being fruitful in every good work, and increasing in the knowledge of God; Strengthened with all might, according to his glorious power, unto all patience and longsuffering with joyfulness;" Colossians 1:9-11 KJV

praise the Lord! ——— ∞ ——— hallelujah!

♥ My Jesus Journal Time! ♥

#96

Let It ALL Go

If there is anyone on this earth who has ever held on for dear life to everything and everyone she was supposed to let go, that was me. I was absolutely the worst at letting go for years upon years. Anything or anyone I was supposed to let go, forget about it. I was way too prideful, way too broken, way too sin-ridden, way too terrified, way too pleasure-driven, way too self-centered, way too self-pitying, etc. to let go. So I held on and held on and held on. Honestly, it's still unbelievably hard for me to let go. But I have learned to let go when I need to IN THE STRENGTH OF GOD – in obedience to God. And I have learned – shockingly – that it's best to TRUST IN THE LORD when He wants us to let go and to BE THANKFUL because His ways and will for us are ALWAYS BEST!

I am thankful He gives me the wisdom I need to know when to let something or someone go, I am thankful for His love, mercy, and patience with me, I am thankful for His perfect will for my life, and I am thankful He gives me all I need to live a godly life – including when it comes to obeying Him in letting go.

This verse below is a huge encouragement to me when it comes to obeying God, and I so hope God will use this message to help you let it ALL go when He tells you to LET GO! Amen!

"According as his divine power hath given unto us all things that *pertain* unto life and godliness, through the knowledge of him that hath called us to glory and virtue:" 2 Peter 1:3 KJV

...

praise the Lord! ———•◦◦◦———— hallelujah!

❤ My Jesus Journal Time! ❤

praise the Lord! ———ooo——— hallelujah!

#97

Totally Devoted – and THANKFUL!

One of the books I have been blessed to write is called *Totally Devoted*. God has impressed upon me over the past few years that this is how He has called His children to be. Totally devoted – to HIM! Sadly, tragically in fact, so much of modern day so-called Christianity and churches in America are filled with outright false teaching as I was under or watered-down, sugar-coated teaching through which people are taught to be lukewarm believers in Jesus. I fell hard for this also for a long time. All of this I found to be self-focused not God-focused. Most importantly it did not line up correctly with the Bible.

Praise God, He led me to repentance, swept me off my feet, drew me away with Him into an about 7-year "wilderness" period of much solitude and time alone with Him, and began by His Holy Spirit to teach me the Bible and how to be a totally devoted follower of the Lord Jesus Christ!

Friend, it's hard, really, really hard on the flesh to deny self of its wishes, ways, and wants when they don't line up with God's ways and will for our lives. But we must pay the price. We must die to self and live for Him. I am more thankful to God than imaginable for not leaving me as yet another casualty of false teaching or of sugar-coated, watered-down teaching. I am so thankful to Him for teaching me daily how to deny myself, take up my cross, and to humbly, faithfully, lovingly, reverently, and devotedly follow His blessed Holy Spirit as He leads me forth!

Are you totally devoted to the Lord Jesus Christ? Please may it be so, friend, and please be thankful to God for the wonderfulness despite the cost of self-denial of being wholly and forever His!

"And he said to *them* all, If any *man* will come after me, let him deny himself, and take up his cross daily, and follow me. For whosoever will save his life shall lose it: but whosoever will lose his life for my sake, the same shall save it." Luke 9:23-24 KJV

"And *that* he died for all, that they which live should not henceforth live unto themselves, but unto him which died for them, and rose again." 2 Corinthians 5:15 KJV praise the Lord! ———•ᴏᴏᴏ———— hallelujah!

♥ My Jesus Journal Time! ♥

#98

Such a Tragic Story

God sent me to a town way up in the northeast portion of America one day that I knew was known for being in the thick of a horrific drug epidemic, but what I witnessed in the only about 30 minutes or so I spent there blew me totally away. You may think I was upset and unthankful God sent me there. But I could not be more thankful to God for sending me there and for what He did through me that day. Sometimes the hardest things God calls us to do, see, hear, watch, experience, etc. are the most incredible opportunities to love, grow, serve, be tested, be purified, give, sacrifice, etc. – and to BE THANKFUL!

The Lord led me to a park with a relatively large number of homeless people all exceedingly high on the same drug. I have been around countless people on drugs in my ministry work and even some who are overdosing and worked with numerous people who are homeless over the years, but this was beyond extreme. There were bodies fallen to the ground, one man appearing to be overdosing, bodies on bodies, other bodies still walking but their limbs entangled, people slumped over, some passed out, and a look of darkness, death, and depravity beyond anything I had ever seen in that many all at once.

One man told me a man had been stabbed nearby and they had found the knife still in him. Another man told me he had stabbed someone but avoided jail. The people, even those awake, looked lightless and lifeless. They looked like zombies not humans.

God gave me the courage to go up to them, and by His love, power, grace, and mercy, I was shocked to find almost all still awake took my *Finding the Light* tracts I offered them which include my personal story and the Gospel message. I was also able to leave tracts by the bodies of those who were unresponsive. I left deeply moved and crying out to God to save them for eternity. I am so, so, so immeasurably thankful to God for entrusting me with loving and giving tracts to and praying for a group of people He created the world has likely given up on. Oh, how I thank God for this!

"For I reckon that the sufferings of this present time *are* not worthy *to be compared* with the glory which shall be revealed in us." Romans 8:18 KJV

praise the Lord! ──────•∞•────── hallelujah!

♥ My Jesus Journal Time! ♥

#99

My Best Friend

In retrospect, as I edit this book and prepare it for publication, I never expected I would have finished up my first draft of the messages on Thanksgiving Day which miraculously was only about the 4th day of writing it. It was a long day of intense writing, and I was so thankful to a long-time friend who dropped off my laundry she had done and some turkey for me. I asked her to set all of it down on and by my car so she wouldn't interrupt my writing when she got to the hotel where I was staying. In her love and kindness, she quietly dropped off the blessings she had for me. As thankful to God as I am for my friend's beautiful and gentle love and sacrifice over the years, she isn't my best friend.

When I was a girl, my supposed best friend at the time who turned out to be anything but gave me a poster about what it means to be a faithful friend. I can't remember a single word on that poster, but I can tell you this. As indescribably humbled and thankful as I am that Jesus Christ is my Lord, God, King, Savior, first love, highest priority, healer, teacher, redeemer, counselor, comforter, helper, master, restorer, advocate, hope, joy, light, and peace, etc., there is something else I want to express my Thanksgiving about regarding my beloved Lord Jesus Christ.

Coming from a background of decades of brokenness beyond human hope, and having had a pretty rough life throughout which I have struggled with one thing or another every day for as long as I can remember even to this very day, and having undergone a miraculous life transformation by the loving heart and hands of God, I have this confession – and Thanksgiving – to proclaim.

The Lord Jesus Christ is my very best friend – forevermore. And I wouldn't have it any other way. He is the very best friend anyone on this earth could ever have. Every day now is a day of Thanksgiving for me. For He is mine and I am His forevermore!

"…and there is a friend *that* sticketh closer than a brother." Proverbs 18:24 KJV

"I *am* my beloved's, and my beloved *is* mine: he feedeth among the lilies." Song of Sol. 6:3 KJV

praise the Lord! ———○○○——— hallelujah!

♥ My Jesus Journal Time! ♥

praise the Lord! ——————ooo—————— hallelujah!

#100
Thanksgiving Forever

I have periodically said over the years that forever will not be enough to thank the Lord. But truth is forever will never end. So those of us who have turned from our sins, believe in Jesus Christ as Lord and in His death and resurrection, who have truly committed our lives to Christ and live utterly for the Lord, will have the opportunity to love, praise, worship, glorify – and THANK THE LORD – forevermore!

As you go forth, may Thanksgiving to the Lord God almighty be part of your very lifestyle. May you be humbly and wholly His. Forever and ever, AMEN!

"Saying, Amen: Blessing, and glory, and wisdom, and thanksgiving, and honour, and power, and might, *be* unto our God for ever and ever. Amen."

. . .

praise the Lord! ———ooo——— hallelujah!

♥ My Jesus Journal Time! ♥

From My Heart to Yours

I am so filled with Thanksgiving to God as I get closer to finishing up the writing and editing and publishing of this latest book God has placed on my heart to write. My life is anything but perfect, I am anything but perfect, this world is anything but perfect, and I could find a zillion reasons as I did for so much of my life thus far to choose to be upset and unthankful.

And that really is what it boils down to, isn't it? We can CHOOSE to look at ourselves and our circumstances and this world and CHOOSE to be down, discouraged, disheartened, depressed, disappointed, downhearted, etc. Or we can CHOOSE to look to the Lord, to the Bible, and to having a relationship with Him now and forever in heaven for those of us who have turned from our sins, believe in Jesus Christ as Lord and in His death and resurrection, and truly turned to God and His ways. And, in so doing, we can choose love, joy, peace, hope, and Thanksgiving to God.

We can CHOOSE to be totally devoted to the Lord and to His ways and His will for us in a world filled with wickedness and countless people with their backs turned to God. We can CHOOSE each and every day to have Thanksgiving in our hearts, in our words, and in our actions. We can CHOOSE God's ways not the world's ways. We can deny self, take up our crosses, and follow Jesus.

And we can CHOOSE to express our Thanksgiving to God as we humbly, lovingly, reverently, devotedly follow the Holy Spirit of God who lives inside His followers as He leads us forth.

As I get closer to finishing up preparing this book to share with all those the Lord leads to it, and as you get nearer to the end of reading and using it however the Lord so leads you, I encourage you with all my heart as I encourage myself to make Thanksgiving a humongous part of our lives for each and every day the Lord gives us on this earth and forevermore! Praise, praise, praise the Lord, AMEN!

love & blessings,

lara

praise the Lord! ———ᵒᵒᵒ——— hallelujah!

About Lara Love

& Good News Ministry

I am a 100% Jewish follower of the Lord Jesus Christ once broken for decades beyond human hope & repair and now overflowing with love, hope, peace & joy on the road for Jesus with my special needs ministry dogs. A writer & evangelist, I write tracts, devotionals, & books and do streets & beach ministry. I also create gifts of t-shirts, cards, mugs, posters and/or anything the Lord desires all as part of my life's calling. My life's calling is to help people become & remain totally devoted followers of the Lord Jesus Christ. Please SIGN UP for my GOOD NEWS DAILY sent by email, visit my ministry, receive help beginning a forever relationship with the Lord & following Him day by day, meet my ministry dogs, and order my tracts, devotionals & books & gifts including my FINDING THE LIGHT Gospel (Good News) tract which includes my personal story at:

Lara Love, Good News Ministry

Telephone: 843-338-2219

www.goodnews.love /// lara@goodnews.love

I am not called by God to communicate by postal mail but am happy to respond to emails & calls. My ministry does not financially sponsor emails & calls. I have a huge heart to love & help all, but need to obey the Lord in this so I am best able to fulfill my calling!

Lara Love, Good News Ministry

PO Box M2 / 3715 Argent Blvd / Ridgeland, SC 29936

Telephone: 843-338-2219

lara@goodnews.love

www.GoodNews.love

Made in the USA
Columbia, SC
10 November 2022

70732843R00120